TRAVELLING
BY TRAIN

THE JOURNEY OF AN AUTISTIC MOTHER

LAURIE MORGEN

Travelling by Train

First published in 2020 by

Panoma Press Ltd
48 St Vincent Drive, St Albans, Herts, AL1 5SJ, UK
info@panomapress.com
www.panomapress.com

Book layout by Neil Coe.

978-1-784529-10-9

Bonnie

There is something in the human soul that looks into the darkest night sky to find just one star, that small light that somehow fills us with hope.

My mystery is the road and I must be ever upon it, aye,
till I can walk no further.

Richard Brome, *A Jovial Crew*

The woods are lovely, dark and deep.

But I have promises to keep,

And miles to go before I sleep,

And miles to go before I sleep.

Robert Frost, *Stopping by Woods on a Snowy Evening*

With warmest wishes

Laurie

TESTIMONIALS

"An eye opener; a 'must read' for any social worker
or professional proclaiming 'children first'.
A heartbreaking true testimony to a parent's love and
dedication that takes them on a journey not chosen
but leading to an outcome that explains so much."

**Dr Wenn B Lawson,
Psychologist AFBPsS; MAPs**

"*Travelling by Train* is far more than a journey of an
autistic mother. It's an incredible insight into how far
someone needed to go to fight against a system hell
bent on ruining her. But, she defies the odds. The
book angered me in parts, made me laugh in others,
but ultimately inspired me in the end."

**Richard McCann,
Times No. 1 Bestselling Author of *Just a Boy***

CONTENTS

INTRODUCTION

What I must do is write. Otherwise nobody will ever know the thoughts, feelings and memories which are both my prison and prisoner. My communication difficulties are subtle yet present, as they are in many autistic people. It makes no sense to others when I am perfectly able to talk, which is all that matters to some. They have no concept of the strangled frustrated voice which runs around like a naughty, petulant inner imp. Unable to understand the subtle nuances of life and language or the culture I had been thrown into by some nasty accident of birth, it despairs. Often unable to articulate myself in meaningful ways, to understand and be understood has been a lifelong source of grief. Perhaps by engaging in written language it will be possible to connect with just one other person and life may be at least a little less solitary. Perhaps my pain and suffering will enable one person to hurt less or heal faster. It would give it some point, some meaning.

When explaining autism, it often proves to be more helpful to describe it as a culture. It seems less intimidating that way, less of a disability. People seem to accept it more easily when attempting to explain the difficulties which arise when someone comes from another country and for whom English is a second language.

I have a dream, a fantasy that my real home is another planet where nobody uses spoken language at all. Our communication is conducted telepathically with meaning and motive losing nothing in the transition from thought to voice, or voice to ear. It's a place of wonderful smells, of forest floor just after rainfall or the throat-warming aroma of new leather and glossy magazines; where everything is comfortable, secure and the lights are never too bright, or too dull. Where I come from, that distant planet, my thoughts are peppered like stars across a midnight sky. Far too many to number, they are there for anyone to see and gaze upon. They can know me and I them, because to understand and be understood across a landscape of acceptance and peace must surely be the finest thing.

In the years since I was diagnosed with Asperger's syndrome, I have often been asked if I think I would have been treated differently if my autism had been known about while I was growing up. The answer is always the same: no. It wouldn't have made my family any kinder. Their belief at the time was that I was mentally ill yet they were still unkind, cruel and at times physically violent and frequently verbally abusive.

Even before I stepped into the psychiatrist's office the first time, at the age of nine, I was labelled. It added reason to be ostracised, bullied and laughed at, especially by my own family. If it wasn't my monotone voice, pedantic speech, obsessive handwashing, strong interests and peculiar habits they ridiculed, it was my tomboy-like attitude and identity. A lack of femininity both in my body shape and attitude were frequent sources of amusement and torment, especially from my mother's side of the family.

As a child, I loved reading Enid Blyton's *Famous Five* books and I, in my fantasy world, modelled myself on George, who was really Georgina. In a world where gender stereotypes were still part of British culture, this rebel child much preferred being outdoors and falling into incredible adventures. George was confident, bold and outgoing. Everything I aspired to be.

Difficulties coping with change caused my family to delay telling me things others had known for a while. My explosive reaction to finally finding out was their prophecy fulfilled. My tearful pleas to be given more notice went unheard. Selfish, jealous, unstable, weak and awkward were labels very often spat at me. I was different, and my mother's family made it absolutely clear this was somehow wrong. Everything which caused me difficulty could have been explained in one word: autism. It wasn't until I was 30 and another psychiatrist told me difference was fine that I began to break away from the misery of trying to be the person my family would accept. It's like being an eternal child, constantly baffled by the surrounding world, its people and how to relate to them.

This book is dedicated to the three young people I love most in the world: my children.

You are among the strongest, most resilient and balanced people I know and I am intensely proud of you.
There are no finer times than those we spend together.
Thank you so much for being the family I always wanted to be part of.

I am Laurie. I am autistic. I am brave, strong and intelligent. This is my journey.

Please take a seat and travel with me.

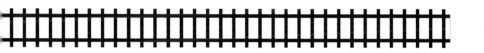

PART I - THE DRIVE

CHAPTER I

We were driving somewhere and I looked across at him, as I often do. The topic of our conversation escapes my memory now but travelling always made a good picnic rug to spread our chatting across. It could have been friendly and jovial banter or a flat discussion over our destination, but it was one of those moments when the realisation of how lucky we both were to be there at all struck me, as it often does, with a flash of amazement and a long, cool river of humility.

He was 16 at the time and the likeness to Mike, his father, stretched across this adolescent's entire presence from his facial appearance to his build and occasional, very slight, almost unnoticeable mannerisms. Had nature been at war with nurture over him, then the victor was obvious in everything about the son of the man I'd loved so intensely. A different kind of writer would have described the changing light across Edmund's strong Arabic features, the music from the van's CD player and the way the landscape changed as our journey ate up miles of motorway while daylight faded into dusk. But I'm not a person to draw vivid pictures of something I can't remember. He was there, my son, that was the most important thing.

Most people get those moments. They see a universe in a blink, an instant where a hundred thoughts and pictures flash a fast rewind, covering years of similar situations. In German, they say *augenblick*, meaning literally *eyes' view*. The almost audible slap of celluloid against the mechanism of the cine projector as the reel comes to an end snaps us back into the present. The roll of film is again stored away in the metal, mental tin of our memories.

We were probably taking the dogs somewhere different that day. They were safe in a pen behind the rear passenger seats. In its former life, it was a breakdown recovery van, bright yellow and easy to find in a car park. It still had a panel of dashboard buttons alluding to its days of noble rescue. To steal a modern day expression, it was my lifestyle option. Good for a keen camper and dog owner. Vandelion, as I called it, could be easily swept clean with a yard brush and mop. There was a deficit of crevices to acquire dog hair and other debris that grind into the velvety upholstery of modern vehicles.

Like my house, the van was rarely clean and hardly ever tidy. It shouted fridge magnet humour: *dull women live in tidy houses*. Perhaps interesting ones were, by default, middle-aged and drove bright yellow vans. Women who liked flicking the switch to turn on the imaginary overhead hazard lights to check they were still present, correct and twirly. When I first bought it, a favourite prank was to show friends those dashboard lights, where each one had a different picture to illustrate its former function. "This one jump starts cars with flat batteries, this one operates the rear hazard lights and this one is for the overhead hazard lights, look," I'd say, pointing to the roof then laugh like a seven-year-old schoolboy when they checked.

My son, how different would our lives have been if you, you giant lump of a teenager with your clumsy walk and dinner plate hands, had been taken away? That was the thought which zigzagged across my consciousness that day. It often did. The thought was there and in a flash was gone again. What kind of family would he have been given to? Would they have been 'respectable', middle-class professionals or an ordinary working couple, infertile and desperate for a baby of their own? Would they have been somehow better equipped to carry on fighting the unjust system which almost took my boy away? Would they have been listened to more seriously than I was when he began to have problems at school? Maybe he would have got his Asperger's syndrome diagnosis earlier. Maybe they would. Or perhaps his later difficulties would have been attributed to his early childhood traumas and blamed, in part, on the mother who wouldn't give up.

Eddy, or more formally Edmund Robin Alexander, was born at home on 25th October 1993. My waters broke to the Eagles' song *Hotel California:* 'Up ahead in the distance, I saw a shimmering light' it went. He was a strong solid baby of eight pounds, six ounces and didn't look like one of mine. His red face and thick dark hair was a sharp contrast to my older two, who had been born blond, fair-skinned and much smaller. They had a different father and although I should have expected my new baby to look different, his red face and dark hair was quite a surprise, but he was handsome.

We spent the rest of the day dozing on the sofa Edmund had been born on. More than once, I looked down at him to check he was real and asleep in my arms. On day three, when my milk came through and hormones went crazy, the familiar tearful day came I'd experienced with the older two children. I sat on the edge of my bed, cradling Edmund and drowning him with tears. I thought of my other two children, living with their father and how much I missed them. As I rocked him, I looked down at the peaceful baby and said, "Nobody is going to take you away from me."

From the birth of Edmund, it was clear that Mike had no idea how to handle a new baby and would often make his son cry. It was his first child and his experience of babies was extremely limited. He often played with him roughly, throwing him up in the air, catching him and twirling him around. Edmund would scream in distress but Mike ignored my pleas to stop. He would, when I said Eddy didn't like it, just say, "Rubbish, he loves it." The ceilings in our late Victorian house were very high and Mike interspersed the throwing game by holding Edmund above his head and twisting him from side to side. As much as I was uncomfortable with this, I tried to balance showing Mike how to hold and play with such a young baby while supporting his interactions with him. It had been clear from Ed's very earliest days that Mike was finding fatherhood a struggle. He seemed to have no concept of appropriate handling, especially when his son cried, and seemed almost jealous of the attention he needed from me. During the night feeds, Mike would hold me tightly, making it difficult to attend to the baby's needs.

Edmund was so very handsome. His dark skin and hair were admired and remarked upon by people we met in the street. The first few weeks went by and a routine started to form. I enjoyed taking him out in the late autumn weather. More than once, a passer-by would say, "He's going to grow up to be a right heartbreaker, that one." I didn't have to wait very long.

It was 4th December, a Saturday evening, when Edmund fell ill. He was five weeks and five days old. For a few days, I'd picked him up in the morning from his cot and found his nightclothes and the bedding around his body damp. In himself, Eddy seemed well enough, although he had been bringing back more feed than usual. My plan was to keep an eye on him over the weekend and take him to see the health visitor on Monday afternoon. Terran and Holly, my older two children, who normally lived with their father, were with us that Saturday. We had all been out with Dave, Mike's younger brother who was visiting from Australia.

That night, I went upstairs to run a bath for the baby. Holly, who had enjoyed the months leading up to her brother's birth, liked to wash and play with him in the bath. Before he had been born, the two of us used to bathe together on the nights she and Terran stayed over. Holly was a sweet and very bright little girl and she liked to wash my tummy. "I'm washing the baby," she would say and then talk to Eddy through my navel, as though it was some kind of human microphone. She came with me to undress and get in the water while I went down to fetch him. Mike and ten-year-old Terran were downstairs with the baby while I settled Holly in the bath. Mike had been vigorously jiggling and trying to pacify his crying baby son, with no luck at all. Ed calmed as soon as I took him from his father's hands.

I took Eddy upstairs where Holly was playing in the bath. I knelt on the floor to undress the baby. The neck opening on his sweater was very tight, which made it difficult to remove. It was when I pulled it over his head that he went limp. He turned into a rag doll, with no muscle tone at all. His complexion had turned grey and his skin suddenly clammy. Had his breath not been coming in loud rasps, anyone would have thought he was dead. Time slowed to a crawl. Ed was clearly unwell. I put him in the bath with his sister, splashing him with water, thinking he would revive. Edmund was unresponsive. It was incredibly difficult balancing a lifeless, larger than average five-week-old baby on my forearm, but I carefully lifted him out of the water and on to a bath towel. His bowels opened spontaneously and a feeling of horror thumped me in the stomach. My actions, thoughts and feelings were at war, pulling away from each other yet sucked at the same time in a tornado of fear and terror. To this day, the memory of it causes feelings of nausea and heart palpitations.

My daughter, just about to turn five, was happy in the bath, unaware of my concern for her little brother. She could have been a continent away, on a different planet or in another world. Her splashes and laughter were a brutal contrast to the limp baby in my arms. Wrapping a clean towel around Edmund's body, I put him on the bathroom floor, safely out of the way. I thought about Mike and how he broke everything. Now he had broken his baby. I shouted for Mike. He came upstairs and took the baby from me. Even he could see something was dreadfully wrong. He passed Edmund back and went to phone a doctor. We had no home phone so it meant walking to a public telephone box.

He came back saying there was no answer so he had called the emergency services and an ambulance was on its way. Holly had dried and dressed herself in pyjamas by the time it arrived. Edmund had revived a little, gaining some colour and had stopped the awful rasping breathing. As a precaution, the paramedic suggested taking him to hospital to be checked over. Mike took Terran and Holly to his mother's house for the night, thinking we all would spend the next day together. I dressed Edmund in a snowsuit to keep him warm and held him in my arms in the back of the ambulance. Why were there no child seat restraints? What if the ambulance crashed? How was a baby held only by its mother ever going to be safe should there be an accident?

At the hospital nothing was making any sense. Everything was surreal, confusing. Edmund was naked on the examination table. Ludicrously happy cartoon picture curtains separated us from the chaos of children's Accident & Emergency and the kid with broken bones sticking out of his leg. Eddy's high-pitched squeal was piercing, painful to hear, heart stopping. Was this my baby? Edmund, my Edmund, wonderful and dark and handsome, was making noises from some black and white Hitchcock film. It was unreal.

He was thoroughly examined by a female doctor who never once looked at me. Her questions were relentless and routine. How long had he been ill? About three or four days. Had he been vomiting? No, just bringing back a little more feed than usual. Had he had any knocks or bumps or been dropped? No, but he had somehow managed to flip himself from his tummy to his back a few days earlier and knocked his head on the floor. She rejected that without turning her head. A baby of that age wouldn't be able to do that. Yet he had, twice. Hadn't I noticed his fontanel was raised? Yes, but I didn't know this was unusual. Edmund had a lot of features alluding to his mixed-race background. How was I supposed to know what was and wasn't normal? Having three children made nobody a paediatrician any more than having monthly periods turned a woman into a gynaecologist.

Although it was by then late at night, children's A&E was packed with injured and ill youngsters. Bright lights, noise, blood, crying children and weeping parents were everywhere. It was somewhere between an abattoir and a fairground. Edmund needed further tests. We had to stay. I was given a fold-out bed to sleep on, in a goldfish bowl cubicle which had glass walls behind more ridiculous curtains. These only partially kept us from the nasty glaring lights of ward E37 and the horrible world beyond. Mike went home. There was no space for both of us.

The couple in the adjacent bay also had a baby son. It was a relief to have somebody to talk to who didn't pound me with relentless questions. They told me their little boy, who was around the same age as Edmund, wasn't feeding properly and was failing to gain weight at home. This was their second or third stay in hospital with him. Worry and the sound of other babies crying made it impossible to sleep. When Mike returned the next day, after taking Terran and Holly home to their father, he brought clothes and a toothbrush with him. It looked as though we were going to be there for some time.

The next few days brought mixed news, some bad and some good. It was contradictory to hear his condition was life threatening but his life wasn't at risk. It made no sense. We were moved to a large private room. Between the Monday after Edmund's admission and the following Thursday, he was subjected to more tests. He had to be X-rayed. They were checking for broken bones. I couldn't understand why they thought he might have any. Mike held Edmund as I couldn't bear to.

The ultrasound scan was taken through Edmund's fontanel, the 'soft spot' at the top of his head. He wriggled and cried until Dr Jaspan, the radiographer, suggested I feed him. It was very uncomfortable having a stranger so close to my breast while I held my baby still. For the MRI scan, Edmund had to be sedated to keep him absolutely still. It brought back memories of the incident in the bathroom when he was unconscious and grey. He looked tiny and everything was tragic yet somehow comical. My baby, on an idiotic supermarket conveyor belt leading him into the open washing machine mouth of the scanner as it took pictures of his brain, slice by slice.

I thought about Trina, a friend whose baby son had died at six months old. As I watched Eddy slowly move into the MRI scanner, I thought about Trina's baby going into the greedy mouth of the furnace at the crematorium, only without the oblong, wedding cake coffin to hug and hold him. Somebody must have ripped her open and torn out her soul when that tiny box, with her dead baby in it, went behind the curtain. She had wailed out loud, filling the gap between the silence in the room and quietly weeping people. She had sung the unspoken, wordless song that now filled my head but couldn't escape from my throat, my soul, my heart.

The staff were very kind. There was a washing machine for parents' use, allowing me to wash our clothes. There was also an endless supply of clean nappies and a cupboard full of children's clothing we could borrow. Mike brought in my camera and I have a photograph of Edmund dressed in one of the romper suits he looked cute in. It said 'Little Artist' on the front. We had use of a big blue coach-built Silver Cross pram we used to rock him in on the ward and transport him to other departments for the endless tests and X-rays. We also took him for walks in and around the hospital and grounds. Even very young babies needed fresh air. Grasping at anything that could establish a new kind of normal, my focus was narrowed to caring for Eddy.

Edmund was found to have bilateral subdural haematomas – bleeding under the skull, on both sides of his brain. Jonathan Punt, a well-known neurosurgeon, was brought in to carry out the treatment. Edmund would need to have a syringe inserted through his fontanel to have the excess fluid drawn off at least every other day. Taps, they called them. I wasn't allowed to be with him for the treatment.

Edmund wasn't going to be sedated for the procedure. He needed to have the hair from the front of his head shaved and be immobilised by wrapping him tightly in a blanket. Somebody would have to hold him still and it was to be Mavis, the nurse allocated to us as a key worker. She lifted Ed out of my arms and took the baby into a treatment room. I waited in the corridor and it was the only time I'd cried since we arrived at the hospital. His shrill screams pierced my numbness.

When he was brought out, I saw through the door the trolley which held the surgical tools. On it were five full specimen bottles of bloodstained fluid. How could all of that have come from one baby head? The bones on his skull were clearly visible and his fontanel was collapsed. He had two stitches, one on either side of his head. Stiff with blood, they looked like the knots in barbed wire. His scalp was stained yellow from the iodine and he looked tiny, fragile. I cannot remember how many times he had the treatment but the fluid they drew off grew less each time. Had it not worked, he would have needed shunts put in his head to draw the fluid away from his brain. These would have needed replacing as he grew.

Time in hospitals works very differently from that of the world outside: never really dark and the temperature on the wards never drops the way it does during the night at home. It was only by the ward orderlies letting themselves into our room at the same time every morning and routine temperature checks that let us know it was another day. We knew night was creeping in when the external windows slowly turned to mirrors, reflecting everything in the room.

I'd been away from the room but not for long, so it was a surprise to see Mavis sitting there. Dr Terence Stephenson, the consultant doctor, was standing by her side. They were solemn and motionless, they could have been a Victorian couple posing for a photograph. It was startling. They told me Edmund had a non-accidental injury. I was confused. In my mind, it was pretty much the same as a non-event. If he hadn't had an accident, then he was ill, would get better and I could take him home. Why then were they saying the police and Social Services were in a room opposite, waiting to interview me? Stunned and with no time to prepare or change my clothes from the old T-shirt I was in to something tidier, I took a long glance across at my son and crossed the corridor. The floor, it felt, had turned into a river racing along the bottom of a canyon.

Years later, Holly reminded me of something I put into a letter to her, that life is like a train journey and we are the train. People join us at different stations along the route and enrich our lives in some way. They are brushstrokes in our lives. We are also part of their journey, passengers on their life train. Each experience is an exquisite interaction which may last for 20 years, or 30, a whole lifetime or no time at all, but everything takes us from where we have been towards the people we are to become. The events over the following months were to become one of those times.

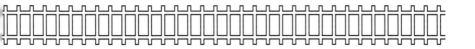

CHAPTER 2

There were two police officers and the same number of social workers in the narrow, windowless room. I sat, in bewildered disbelief, on the low chair between them. There was no way of knowing whether or not they were friendly or hostile until their questions began. The social workers, Anne O'Connor and Ashley Slater, explained that Edmund's injury was non-accidental – that word again. All the tests, the X-rays, scans and examinations had been to establish a cause but there was none. As a result, the conclusion of medical opinion was he had been shaken. I wanted to know by whom. Who would hurt a small baby?

The police and social workers both asked the same questions. Had Edmund been left alone with anyone? Only me and his father, they heard. How long had he been ill? I didn't know he was ill. Had I noticed anything unusual about him? Only that he had been bringing back more feed than usual for a few days. Hadn't I noticed his fontanel was raised? No. Edmund had a lot of hair and it was difficult to tell. Besides which, how was it possible for me to necessarily know what was normal for a mixed-race baby?

What was my relationship with his father like? I loved him. He was my soulmate. We had fallen out quite often during my pregnancy because he was out of work and I was worried about money. Why hadn't I taken him to the doctor sooner? I'm not the kind of person to hurry off to the doctor over every little thing. The same questions I'd been asked time and again over the past few days.

If I was open and honest with them, they said, it would go in my favour. In that dark cave of a room and too shocked to think straight, I tried my best. Maybe, once I'd answered their questions, I would be able to go home. It was getting close to Christmas. Since my separation from their father, I'd always celebrated Christmas a day early with my children, so they could be home with their father and wake up as they always had, with presents to unwrap from the wider family. We had been looking forward to spending the time together.

That day, 9th December, Holly was five. The indignation this was happening on her birthday stung hard. It was supposed to be a fun day, where she got treats and an outing, a special time where everything was about her as it had been the year before. I left the hospital to go and see her, buying a cuddly toy on the way as it was all I had time to buy. It was a nasty contrast to the previous year, when she spent the whole day with me, when we went to choose a special present from the toy shop walking distance from my house. As nothing in the shop was over £25, she was allowed to pick anything, which excited the four-year-old girl. She circled around the shop, dancing over this toy and that and she took on a special voice, the one which was always accompanied by her eyes growing round when they spied something delicious, "Oh, Mummy, can I have this?"

Turning from the display of wall clocks, I then saw what her hand was resting on. It was the biggest rocking horse imaginable and her little hand could barely reach its back. It cost over £300 and was something I'd forgotten about. I laughed and said, "Sweetie,

THE JOURNEY OF AN AUTISTIC MOTHER

I would love to buy you that one but it's just a little bit too much money. They sell hobby horses, why don't you pick one of those? You'll be able to ride it wherever you like." It was good enough for her so we chose one, along with a Winnie the Pooh wall clock. The cartoon bear was holding a big balloon which was the clock face, his body being a pendulum which swung from side to side as the clock ticked.

She rode the hobby horse home and I carried the clock. We had arranged to meet my sister and her two daughters later on so Holly had time to play at home. Somehow, we managed to get her and her presents on the back of my bicycle to ride the four miles to McDonald's in the town, which lay between my house and Jane's. A senior member of staff realised it was somebody's birthday; she took Holly off to the upstairs of the restaurant, returning her a few minutes later with party bags and hats for the children.

A year on and I sat on Derek's sofa, telling him about my interview with the police and Social Services. He had a new partner and they were as impassive as I was numb about the whole situation. They offered no advice and I didn't ask for any. Over time, they became increasingly judgmental and more difficult to deal with.

A meeting was to be arranged regarding Edmund's welfare and the social workers advised me not to take him out of the hospital. I'd previously been able to walk him in the ward pram around the local area; we both needed fresh air and time away from the hot, dry and bright hospital was good. We had even done some Christmas shopping. Although I was free to come and go as I pleased, it was uncomfortable leaving Edmund on his own on the ward. If he needed anything, would anyone attend to him promptly? Practically speaking, it was never easy leaving a breastfed baby for long anyway.

I took to walking the hospital corridors. It broke the boredom and monotony of the self-imposed imprisonment. Nobody would have tried to persuade me otherwise if I'd left him there and gone home. When my older children came to visit, it gave them something to do, to walk with me around the building. During the five weeks we were in the hospital, we got to know those floors very well.

Mum was a regular visitor, bringing supplies of disposable nappies and toiletries for both of us. My sister often brought her daughters, along with my children and younger brother David. It was hard trying to keep a sense of normality and privacy was almost impossible to achieve. Mike stayed over most nights, bringing in toys for Edmund and different clothes for me. We slept in a fold-out bed but were often woken in the mornings by orderlies bringing in cups of tea. They didn't seem to know how to knock at the door first. Once or twice we went out to a local pub after Edmund had been fed, bathed and settled into bed.

It was a strange sensation, entering the meeting room. Hospital staff and the two social workers I'd met a few days earlier were at the large boardroom type table, as was my health visitor from home. I felt like Alice, after taking from the bottle labelled 'drink me'. Everyone else looked very smart, businesslike and professional. Unprepared for that foreign situation, my clothes were scruffy and inadequate. I felt very, very small. There was hardly any room at the table. It was all so disproportionately large and absurd and I felt very tiny, almost in need of a ladder to climb on to the chair.

Every head was a nodding balloon, faceless, intimidating. The language was strange, filled with terminology I didn't understand. These people were well rehearsed and prepared. To me it was unknown, alien and frightening but optimism at taking Edmund home after the meeting fuelled a dying hope. Following the proceedings was impossible. I didn't know how he became injured and could add no more to what had already been said. It was a burble, like the sound of speech as heard from underwater while watching a million games of table tennis.

Edmund was placed under an interim care order and put on the child protection register. Effectively, he was in the care of the local authority. Darkness continued to creep in like the lengthening shadow of a winter's nightfall. No longer could I take Edmund unaccompanied off the ward. Someone of authority had to come too. He wasn't going to be coming home. The hospital staff agreed to keep him until after Christmas and it was only later I learned this was to enable him to spend his first and maybe only Christmas with me. The mechanism of a system was in place, its greasy cogs moving slowly towards foster care and finally adoption.

Maybe it was at this meeting that it became apparent that Edmund was going to be the subject of childcare proceedings. They were saying someone had deliberately hurt my baby but I'd no idea who. The Social Services pounded me for information but I'd already told them everything: Mike handling Edmund very roughly but no, he hadn't lost his temper with him. He was jealous, it seemed, of the attention a small baby needed and would often hold on to me in bed, trying to prevent me from getting up for the night feeds. At times, it was like having two children and he behaved more like a displaced older sibling than a father.

My suggestion that it was an accident was rubbished. They said whoever did it knew it but they didn't know Mike. He was careless and clueless, but deliberately causing Edmund's injury? I wouldn't accept that. I knew him and knew how he broke everything. I kept to myself the thought from the night in the bathroom, when Edmund had gone into a state of collapse. The image of placing my baby, wrapped in a towel, in the corner of the bathroom and thinking 'oh Mike, you broke your baby' were words never spoken out loud to anyone.

I was almost grateful Edmund was being placed on the child protection register. The Social Services said if we were open and honest with them it would go in our favour and they could work with us. Maybe they could help Mike to understand the needs of babies and deal with them more appropriately. What I came to realise was 'open' and 'honest' was one-sided and relied on an admission of guilt, that the perpetrator should own up to it. Had I hurt Edmund, I would have said so and told them the same. At the time, I was too naive to realise that had I done so would have meant his immediate removal from my care. Anything which meant taking him home I would have done. Secrecy and deceit had never been strong points with me and it wouldn't have been possible to have lied.

We were advised to seek legal advice and Mike found a solicitor. In a letter, my father was very strong in his opinion and urged me to get my own. He said it was a sad, sick situation and urged me to get out of it but I was already trapped. If nobody admitted to causing Edmund's injury, then no one could work with us. My religious beliefs held on to a fragile hope that forgiveness and kindness would encourage Mike to confess to an act which I'd not seen. He had got up in the night on a couple of occasions when the baby was crying and sleepless. Perhaps he had shaken him just a little, to calm him down?

We started to argue. I tried to persuade Mike to confess to causing the injury but neither could he admit to something he hadn't done. Some months later, I read his own statement to the police. In it he made what is known as a partial confession. He admitted he 'must have done it (caused the injury) because she (me) wouldn't do something like that'.

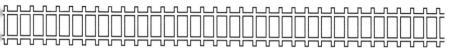

CHAPTER 3

Terran and my ex-husband had both been interviewed by the police and Social Services. They wanted to know if I'd been prone to outbursts of temper while I was living there, had my parenting ever been brought into question? Had Terran seen either Mike or me act violently towards Edmund? At ten years old he was deemed able to tell someone what he had seen.

By this time, my story of Edmund becoming ill in the bathroom, when I pulled his jumper over his head, was being refuted. But it was true and why didn't they ask Holly? She was almost five and wasn't considered reliable. I couldn't understand why they would discount what I said. I wasn't saying pulling a jumper over Edmund's head had created the injury but had created sufficient pressure to cause his loss of consciousness. Nobody seemed to believe me. They'd almost expected me to notice he was seriously ill and take him to the doctor straight away.

They pointed out he had one eye that didn't open as wide as the other. He had been born like that. Nobody was listening. Edmund couldn't open either eye when he was born as they were stuck down tight. He was covered in so much of the thick white vernix that it took almost a week to bathe it out of his armpit and neck creases and two days before his eyes were fully open. In that time, he had been seen by the doctor and midwife. Nobody raised any concern so why would I?

Edmund, although my third child, was very different from the other two: he was mixed race. Mike's father was Algerian. Even when the doctor came for a routine visit when the baby was a few days old and pointed out the blue spots on Edmund's buttocks, I thought nothing of it. These are very common birthmarks among darker skinned people, especially those of Asian, East Indian and African descent. These spots can be, and often are, mistaken for bruises, as I later found out.

Things like this only happened to other people, who knew what to say, what to do, how to beat the system and cheat the rules. All I knew was how to look after Edmund and keep as much as possible to the routine he would have had at home. Routine was important to babies and so was continuity of care. Apart from the few times I went out, I never left him. Either Mike or I bathed him at night, read him stories and played with him. Friends and family were supportive, visiting regularly. My sister brought Terran and Holly to see us; they made get well cards and played with their brother. Mum brought disposable nappies and David, my brother, often kept me company, as did members of the informal church which had been meeting in our house right up until Edmund was taken into hospital. Dad came by a few times; one visit coincided with Mike's family being there, including his brother Dave who was visiting from Australia and staying with his mum.

It was uncomfortable having so many people in the room at one time. With the exception of these visitors, I was cut off from the rest of the world, the real one, where I knew how to live, what to think. All of that safety and familiarity was no longer there; simple things, like grocery shopping, my weekly swimming session, having people stop me in the street to admire my baby. "Isn't he dark and hasn't he got a lot of hair?" were their usual exclamations.

During this time, Dad wrote me a letter concerning the situation we were in. He told me it was a 'sad, sick situation' and I had to get out. He didn't say how, or what I was supposed to do. He also urged me to get my own solicitor in case Mike and I separated but also to add weight and power to our case. Taking his advice on this, I went to see Fay, who was a partner in a law firm close to where I lived. She specialised in family and criminal law and, although we had lost touch, we had known each other for about 17 years. In fact, she came to my wedding when Derek and I were married. Sitting in her office under such circumstances was awkward. We caught up on some news while I explained my situation to her, which seemed to make more sense to her than it did to me. It was a relief to know there was a professional person on board.

Fay, Terry and I, along with Paul, who was also at my wedding, were the youngest members of Nottingham Writers' Club. Paul had been a lecturer in social sciences at what was then known as Trent Polytechnic and I learned a while later that he had taught Ashley Slater. After Terran was born, my attendance at the writers' club dropped off and each of us went on to do other things. Paul married one of his former students and moved to Dundee. Terry went to university and became an English teacher.

It was a difficult enough meeting but hearing about my old friends' progression and Fay's very happy remarriage in the light of what was happening to me added more pain to my frayed self-esteem. I returned to the hospital without even calling in at home. There was no one there. Mike had come down to see his own solicitor and we travelled back together. What little we saw of the town looked bleak and inhospitable. People were working, shopping, living, and unaware of the tragedy unfolding in the lives of this family, the ripples of which were spreading outwards.

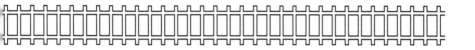

CHAPTER 4

Anne O'Connor, the Social Services manager, came to see me on Christmas Eve. We sat in the same room as we had at the initial interview. It was almost a cruel psychological trick to choose this particular time. She asked me the same questions I'd heard before and would hear again so many times. Had I lost my temper with Edmund? No. If I'd not caused Edmund's injury, what were my feelings towards Mike? I loved him, I told her that. She said if I was open and honest it would go in my favour. They could work with us. Nothing made any sense. I was being as open and honest as I could.

Had I seen Mike hurt Edmund? No. I would have said so. He handled him very roughly at times and didn't know how to look after a baby but I'd never seen him shake Edmund. The force used against him had been severe and whoever had done it would have known about it. Mike hadn't been violent with either of us. His behaviour could be inappropriate but he wasn't violent. He would often try to stop me from getting out of bed in the night to go and feed Edmund. Sometimes he would swear at him but I never saw him angry with him.

Had anyone else been left alone with him? No. Had my elder son, Terran, handled him at all? I was shocked at the implication. My children were never left on their own with Edmund for more than a few minutes. Was she suggesting that my son would pick up his baby brother, shake him violently and put him back in the time it took for me to go to the toilet? My elder son was small for his age and even picking Edmund up was a challenge. He wouldn't have been physically capable of lifting a baby over his head to shake him and had never been impatient with his brother.

I was sure this unexpected, unannounced visit was unethical but I was trapped, desperate and trying to be helpful. Somehow, I thought it would mean this whole nightmare would soon go away and Edmund could go home. This was implied many, many times by the various social workers we were to meet. Their mantra was *if you are open and honest with us it will go in your favour; if you are open and honest with us we can work with you.* Here I was, in hospital with my baby on Christmas Eve, sitting opposite a woman, a social work manager, a stranger. She was asking questions which piled confusion on to post-natal hormones.

It seemed such a contradiction: my baby had a life-threatening injury although his life wasn't at risk. He had been put on the child protection register and neither Mike nor I could take him off the ward. And she was asking me what my feelings towards Mike were. He was my friend. He told me I was beautiful. We were soulmates. Why would he deliberately hurt our baby? "I don't know," said Anne O'Connor, "maybe you can tell us?" I couldn't.

Mike, who had been dividing his time between being at the hospital and spending time with his mother, brother, sister and her partner, came over later on. As many children as possible had been sent home. Edmund clearly wasn't one of them. This wasn't the way his first Christmas should have been. Terran and Holly had been to see us and had opened their presents in our room. The contrast between this Christmas and the year before was as stark a contrast as the relentlessly bright hospital lights and parching dryness of the heat. I wasn't on the rota to work and had fetched the children across on Christmas Eve. Effectively, it gave the children time with me and left Christmas Day to spend at home. I remembered that day well.

One of the line managers at work liked to go shooting and had given me a duck and a pheasant which came frozen and with feathers, head and feet intact. They looked like feathery skittles and took up most of the space in the freezer. We removed the duck to thaw ready for our Christmas dinner. Holly, who had recently turned four, fell in love with the duck, a male mallard, and carried it around the house, cradling it in her arms, stroking the feathers. Mike had a wonderful rapport with my daughter. He was as good with small children as he was bad with babies and both of my children got on really well with him. He was fun, boyish and spoke to them on an easy level.

"Give me the duck," he said, taking the bird out of Holly's hand. He held it by its middle and pointed it over the sofa, which was in the middle of the living room. "Fly to freedom bird, fly, fly!" he said, and threw the duck over the back of the sofa. It fell with a solid thud on the wooden floor. Holly squealed with laughter. We all did.

That Christmas seemed so very long ago. Mike and I turned out the light, folding against each other as we always did. Against the world and its craziness and to the sound of hushing hospital noises, we went to sleep.

Any parent who has a child in hospital at Christmas must feel similar emotions to those shared by Mike and me. We were glad Edmund was better; he was happy and oblivious to the surroundings. The little stocking left by night staff on the corner of his cot contained a few small toys. Edmund had presents from the family so Mike and I opened them with him. One of the toys in the gift stocking was a fur-covered rubber duck. It looked innocent enough, almost cute, but it quacked gruffly when its tummy was squeezed. Edmund hated it. He liked the musical light we got for him, and from then on he went to sleep lulled by the gentle tune and the light show of nursery rhyme animals dancing a rainbow across the ceiling.

He was now exactly two months old and had spent three weeks on the ward. It seemed somewhere between forever and an endless nightmare. Where would we be next Christmas? Lurking beneath the seasonal cheer was the chilling thought Edmund might not be with us for another.

Mike was spending Christmas dinner with his family so he left to join them shortly after we had opened Edmund's presents. At some point, I'd brought an old bicycle across from home and it was this I used to travel over later on to join them all. Before then, more visitors came around the ward. Professor Stephenson, dressed in a Santa Claus costume, walked down the ward with a sack of toys. More toys, more kindness. The whiskered smile he gave me was warmer than a Caribbean sun and kept the faint light of hope burning. Maybe everything would be all right after all.

There was another meeting, the result of which was much clearer this time. As nobody had admitted to injuring Edmund, he was to be placed in local authority care. It was devastating and unreal. I'd no idea how this could be happening to me. I didn't understand what was going on, or the mechanism of the system setting it all in place. If there was ever a need for someone to have an independent advocate, this would have been the time.

Edmund was being kept in hospital until a foster placement could be found. We would be allowed to see him, spend time with him, but not on our own. He couldn't go home. Further assessments would be made to evaluate our parenting skills, we were told, which made us believe this was a test to pass. Once we had done so, we would be allowed to take Edmund home. A Guardian ad Litem had been appointed, who was there to speak for Edmund as he was under ten years old and unable to voice his own opinions. He was also given a solicitor. We had no choice in this and couldn't speak to him, yet both of these people were supposed to be acting 'in his best interests'. That they could do this without consulting his parents shocked us.

As far as Edmund's care and daily routine were concerned, everything was much the same as usual. It was as though Mike and I were, however, looking over a bottomless canyon just before being pushed. In the confusion, he was all I had that was consistent. We clung on, each one the other's life raft.

Before he went away, we wanted Edmund dedicated so I visited the hospital chaplain, who arranged a short but very personal service. Unlike those often found at ordinary church dedications and baptisms, the service sheet had Edmund's name on it. The chaplain also gave us a personalised card. It was only afterwards that he told us most children he saw were dying and he made the services personal to comfort the family. A few friends came along. One of them brought his guitar and later we all sat around in Edmund's room, singing and filling the ward with music, but our laughter couldn't warm the deep chill of fear drawing its clammy fingers across my back.

A foster home had been found, still in the borough we lived in but in another town. We prepared to leave hospital. Edmund's clothes and toys were packed away in two black bin liners; most of them would go with him to give him at least a little familiarity. I bought a breast pump to express my milk for him. He was still only 11 weeks old and I wanted him to continue to get the best nourishment possible.

It was Ashley Slater, our social worker, who took us over to the foster home. They were a married couple and the man had been a town councillor. Very respectable, I thought, nice, upstanding members of the community and far better placed, I thought with full irony, to look after my baby than his parents. They were given my handwritten, detailed instructions on Edmund's day to day care and routine. He hadn't been separated from me before as I'd spent every night with him from birth, right through his hospital stay, up to that point. Everything I'd ever read about baby care stressed the importance of establishing a routine.

Mike got into an argument with the foster carers, which was understandable but unhelpful. I'd already been crying and was trying to give Edmund one last feed before leaving. Ashley witnessed everything; it almost looked as though the verbal altercation was going to turn into a physical fight and the last thing I wanted.

We had seen Edmund during the day at a local Family Support Centre, under the supervision of their staff. He'd be collected in the morning by a volunteer driver and returned in the afternoon. I was welcome to meet Edmund from the foster home and see he was returned but Mike wasn't, on account of the previous argument. A place in a mother and baby home had been found but Edmund would stay with the foster family for two weeks until funding and other practicalities had been made.

To maintain contact with his half-siblings, it was organised for Terran and Holly to see Edmund on Saturday afternoons until we moved. Everything about this was dreadful; the visits were to be in a children's home close to the foster carers' house. There were hardly any toys for the older children to play with and the two hours we had together dragged. We were all bored; the tiny basement room smelled of damp and the atmosphere was depressing. There was nowhere to put Edmund, so he spent the whole time in my arms, which made reading to Holly very difficult.

A social worker had been appointed to supervise the time we were there and sat so close we were almost touching. Outside the room there were trees which blocked out what little winter sun there was. It gave the place a haunted, desolate feel. I came away feeling soiled and ashamed, guilty for the way in which my three children, especially Terran and Holly, had no choice in the awful environment. However, it was important to cooperate and show the authorities I was a good mother and capable of looking after children, even under this humiliation.

The two weeks Edmund was in the foster home were uncomfortable, with much of the memories lost. They treated my baby as their own and seemed to resent me being there, although they appeared to feed Edmund with the breast milk I expressed and froze to pass on to them. The foster carers only looked after babies and had their own store of clothes, which Edmund wore even though they were too small. It worried me the all-in-one suits were pulling on his toes but the concerns I voiced went unheard. He was a big baby and at 12 weeks needed clothing to fit a six- to 12-month-old child.

With hindsight, I should have just taken them off him and not given them back until we moved into the mother and baby home, but being 'open, honest and cooperative' was foremost in my mind. We were quietly bullied into compliance with the promise it would look better for us.

It was also extremely uncomfortable to have been robbed of an active part in Edmund's care. The social workers had been accusing me of not putting 'Edmund's best interests' first. By this they were implying that I put Mike first. They were also saying, which was expressed at the magistrates' court hearing, that one or both of us had caused the injury. There was still no admission of guilt and this seemed to be an excuse to disregard my feelings. They wanted us to help them but it meant they gave nothing, didn't listen and took everything away.

It seemed designed to be disempowering; we answered their questions and I, at least, was always as open as I could be, probably giving away too much information, but desperation to get Edmund back overrode everything else. I would have done anything to achieve it, anything apart from lie. It was a fruitless, eternal circle. Mike couldn't or wouldn't admit to hurting Edmund. We were assured the three-month assessment at the mother and baby home would be to see how competent we were as parents. I believed it was just a process to pass through. Nobody had ever raised doubts about my childcare before and they would be happy with it now. It was just a matter of time.

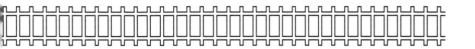

CHAPTER 5

St Joseph's was a row of houses joined together and originally belonged to the Catholic Church. When it was set up, by an order of nuns, it was 'a home for unmarried mothers'. Here they would learn baby care, budgeting, cooking skills and everything else necessary to become good little housewives. Once the terrible stigma of pre-marital sex resulting in a baby had been fully repented of, they were free to shed the sackcloth of their shame and chastened, rejoin polite and respectable society.

By the time Edmund, Mike and I arrived, St Joseph's had come under the control of Nottinghamshire Social Services, and although we lived in Derbyshire, a place was found to enable our assessment to take place. It was fairly apparent, even to us, that Ashley Slater and Anne O'Connor were mildly irritated by this as they held out no hope for Edmund's future with us and would have preferred it if he had simply been placed for adoption. It was only on the insistence of the magistrates at a recent court hearing that forced them into looking for an alternative.

A place became available and we moved in on 24th January that year. Edmund was by then three months old. It was a relief to get Edmund away from the foster home and the too-tight clothing and look forward to seeing Terran and Holly in a less hostile environment than the dark and cold basement of the abandoned children's home.

Our room was up a set of stairs to the right of the front door and overlooked the back of the house. There was a double bed, for no good reason at all because partners were not allowed to stay. The cot was in front of a sash window which lifted up fully. Below it there was a flat conservatory roof which became something of an escape. At times, when I wanted privacy, I would climb out of the window and on to the roof for a cigarette. The front bedroom was empty but soon to become a temporary home to a pregnant woman and her two-year-old son. Both rooms shared a small landing and bathroom. One side of the room was wall to wall fitted wardrobes, and to the right of it a narrow alcove stretching the length of half the room and had a row of kitchen units, a sink, a kettle and baby bath.

We were told the rules which had to be followed or we could lose the placement, which would have put Edmund back with foster carers. It was an unnecessary intimidation. Mike and I weren't allowed to take the baby out unsupervised until after our first review, when half an hour would be granted if everything went well – if we were good, well behaved and obedient, perhaps. Any injuries to Edmund, however mild, had to be reported and shown to the staff on duty, noted, remarked upon and judged. If the explanation given was in any way inadequate, we would have to go with him to hospital. Edmund's bath time had to be carried out under staff supervision. All residents were to take part in household chores such as cleaning the toilets, visitors' area, laundry and corridors. These were allocated in weekly residents' meetings, as were the weekly accompanied shopping trips. Two of us could go and we had to take turns.

The aim was to help parents learn to shop and prepare meals for their families. Although vaguely patronising, it was a good way to get out of the unit and as it was supervised, the benefit was obvious to me more than some of the others, who had either no inclination to visit a supermarket or they had enough free time out of St Joe's anyway. As a result, Ed and I got to go a disproportionate number of times. One person, or couple, was to plan and cook lunch for all the residents, when we were expected to sit at the tables in the large kitchen/diner at the front of the house and eat together. We were left to organise our own evening meals. There was a ground floor smoking room for staff and residents. Fathers were allowed to stay between 10am and 10pm and were also expected to take part in housework duties and care of their children. This was essential if their parenting skills were also to be judged.

I had to hand over my benefit book, as the social security payments I received contributed to the placement. As we also got tokens for free milk, mothers who didn't use them could sell them to St Joseph's. Edmund was once again being breastfed so it was a small way to get some extra money. Later on, I learned I was the only person in the memory of staff there who didn't buy formula milk. As the money returned to us had to be used for buying nappies, baby food and personal items, it didn't always stretch very far but we could use food that was bought in the weekly shop. This is how I would cook Edmund's dinners. All of my children had been weaned on home cooking, and over a period of time I showed the other mothers how to cook and process meals for their babies.

Seeing the deputy manager brought some hope. Sandy was a young woman who had been part of the group of young Christians who had visited my house each week a few years earlier. I was married to Derek and Terran had been our only child. She was insipid and had suffered bulimia herself but had witnessed my parenting of a young child. Sandy would know I wasn't dangerous. She had known me when I was respectable, married and ordinary. How long had I been trying to be normal? To be the kind of person, girl, woman my mother would like? It was an impossible burden to carry and I sat on the side of the bed, crying. I needed air.

Dressing Edmund in the one-piece yellow and blue snowsuit Mum had bought, I put him in his pushchair and went outside. The garden was enclosed by a waist-high brick wall. It was a naked paddock of space, the square expanse of grass with one solitary tree at the bottom. Like the vacant void of my soul, it yearned for life. It was too rutted to push the pushchair around, so instead I pulled it behind me, in a furious, circular walk, and stopped for a cigarette as far from the house as possible. Rebellion burned my soul, consumed with hatred for the situation I was in. Nobody followed me because it was late January and cold. The garden was visible from the office. Should anyone have wanted to witness my furious walk, they could have watched through the window.

Below the tree I found a fallen branch, which brought me back to reality and I took it inside. Over the next few days, I decorated it with anything shiny I could find. Sweet papers and other small objects were dangled on sewing thread to make a mobile for Edmund. I named it the 'Eccentricitree' and wedged it between the radiator and his cot. He loved it. He soon learned that if he kicked both of his legs downwards, as he lay in bed, it would make the tree shake and the decorations flutter. There are few things better than hearing babies laughing and Edmund's giggles were a total pleasure, a reality in an unreal world.

Protests from the other residents came the next day. They were complaining about my breastfeeding of Edmund in the day room. Staff asked me to use the residents' lounge at the back of the house because I was allegedly 'getting my tits out' in front of their men. Had I been drunkenly dancing semi-naked on the table, it would have made sense, but I was a minority among ignorant attitudes so had to comply. The only common factors between me and the others were we were all parents of young children and all under assessment. Not all of the children had been injured. They may have come from homes where domestic violence, drug or alcohol abuse was the norm. Many of them had been poorly educated.

Everyone had a different 'care' plan and mine was the only one that prohibited unsupervised outings with their child. It seemed unjust but the other mothers were more clever than me. They came from backgrounds who knew how to work the system, to make the right noises to the right people and eventually take their children home. They pretended they'd separated from their partners, given up drugs or were eager to keep a more wholesome and secure lifestyle. They claimed their children now came first, that the fathers were bastards, who would never have contact with them over as many dead bodies as it took to convince staff of their sincerity. Had staff been around in the residents' lounge, the kitchen or smoking room, they would have heard quite different stories.

Not everyone was like this. The woman who took the room on the same landing as me arrived shortly after I did, heavily pregnant and with a two-year-old son who only ever squealed 'no'. In all the months we were there together, nobody heard the little boy ever say anything else. Apparently, he had been able to talk but the trauma of seeing his mother constantly beaten by his father had robbed him of all speech, apart from that one word. I liked her. Sarah was different from the other mothers. Intelligent and friendly, she was genuinely warm towards her son and very involved with him. She played with him, sang and read stories, everything I did with my own children; they were the kind of things loving homes were built upon.

Occasionally, her husband would visit. He came to see his son; Sarah had left him because of his violence but he was allowed contact with little Gwyn. They played together in the day room while Sarah stayed in her room. We rarely spoke but she was quiet towards everyone and I have wondered many times since what became of their lives and that of the baby girl we heard she had given birth to after she left the home.

As with any new arrival, there was always a lot of initial activity, such as registering with the local doctor and visiting the baby clinic, which we did the day after arriving at St Joe's, as the residents called it. Still bewildered by the change of routine and environment, I found the clinic noisy and invasive. I refused to sit next to the staff member who accompanied me and instead sat on a chair as far away from the other parents as possible with my back to them, cradling Edmund and rocking him from side to side. He had to be examined and undressing him yet again in front of another stranger, as had happened frequently in hospital, made me feel sick. Was there ever going to be any privacy, dignity or respect for us?

Ashley Slater, our social worker, and Paul Hillingwood, Edmund's Guardian ad Litem, would visit. They would spend time in the office, talking to the staff before seeing us. It felt as though they were all co-conspirators in a master plan to rob us of Edmund. In their language, he 'presented as a white British baby'. Were they a commodity to be bought and sold, white British babies would have fetched the highest price as they were the least likely to be placed for adoption. This was denying him the right to know of his mixed-race origins and we presumed potential adoptive parents wouldn't have been told of his Algerian/Welsh heritage and the family stories which get passed down through generations, the ones young children love to hear again and again.

Mike and I grabbed what time together we could. We took as much advantage of the Thursday night babysitting service as we were able. A male volunteer would cycle over for a couple of hours so two mothers could go out. When it was our turn, Mike and I devised a game to add a fun element to the nights out. After Edmund was bathed, fed and in bed, I'd get ready and leave. I would walk along to a nearby pub, buy myself a drink and sit down. Mike would stay behind for ten or 15 minutes and would go to the same pub, buy a drink for himself and look around, see me and wander casually over. We pretended not to know each other. He would chat me up and I would flirt. After buying me another drink, we would leave together, walk around for a while and have sex underneath a fire escape behind a row of shops. The freedom from the stress we were both under and the risk of being caught added to the moment. The possibility of being discovered was exciting. We also found quiet areas around the mother and baby home to have quick knee tremblers and this way managed to maintain a reasonably regular sex life.

There were also many nights at St Joseph's he would pretend to leave and then slip up the stairs so we could spend the night together. In the morning, he would leave through the sash window of my room, on to the conservatory roof, slide down the drainpipe to the ground and ring the front doorbell to be let in. It meant locking the door to my room because the waking night staff would look in. Nothing in the staff handover book ever said 'Door checked (time). Locked. No staff access'. What were they expecting to find? Parents who were in the throes of suffocating their children? No amount of close supervision would have prevented anyone from harming their baby, as I found out.

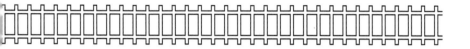

CHAPTER 6

A mother of a two-year-old boy and baby girl came to St Joseph's shortly after me. I cannot remember how long she was with us for but one day we were told she was at hospital with her children. She was missing for hours and came home alone. Her children had been taken away. It was that easy. The reaction among the other residents was indifferent but to me it was menacing. Her son had been found to have fingernail scratches down one of his cheeks, allegedly inflicted by his mother. She was allowed to stay for a few days and then left. I never knew where she went, but her children, I was later told, were adopted by a childless couple who lived on a farm.

Shortly after this, Edmund had an appointment with the doctor for some vaccinations. Our health visitor took us, which was quite a relief as it meant I could still have the half an hour unsupervised outing with my baby later on that day, but we never got it. As usual, Edmund had to be stripped and examined. I noticed red marks where his socks had been and innocently pointed them out. The skin was unbroken, they were neither cuts nor grazes and didn't seem to be causing any pain to Edmund.

The health visitor noted them to the doctor, who declared that type of red mark couldn't have been caused by socks, even though they'd been tight, and we were to go to the local children's Accident & Emergency unit. Beside myself with fear, I was frightened that Edmund would be taken away. The recent memory of the other mother, along with that of Edmund's first visit there when his head injury was diagnosed, was horrific. No plausible explanation was found but we were allowed to go back to St Joseph's. Much was made of this incident and it was debated about in court many months later.

Edmund sustained other minor injuries during our stay at St Joseph's, some of which I witnessed and others I didn't. Only one other time led to a hospital visit but the others were easily explained. He got a bruised foot. I left him with Mike while I went to the local shop for cigarettes and was gone for no more than ten minutes. Immediately, I took him to the office and presented him to the duty staff. I said he did it while I was holding him and he got his foot caught in my belt. They believed me.

On another occasion, he was teething and grumpy. It was lunchtime so Mike looked after him while I ate. Apparently, he was on a play rug, lifted his head and then banged his nose on the floor. Still believing the Social Services would work with us and teach Mike how to handle a young baby appropriately, I was complicit in the untruths of these very minor injuries. He still had little idea how to care for Edmund but I wrongly trusted the supervision would offer some guidelines. No. St Joseph's didn't provide any structured advice or classes in baby care of any kind. What residents had was through informal chats with staff.

One injury, which Edmund still has the scar for, happened one evening while Mike was bathing him. As always, we were being watched by a member of staff, who failed to record my anxiety and request for Mike to remove his studded wristband in case it injured Edmund, which it duly did, as I pointed out. I had a doctor's appointment the next day. Edmund was fed, had his nappy changed and was settling into an afternoon nap when I left him. I told the duty staff and was gone for little more than half an hour.

When I came back, I was called into the office for a confrontation. They alleged Edmund had needed another nappy change and was found to have 'scratches all over his back and bruising on his bottom'. They'd undressed Edmund and given him a full body examination in my absence. "They aren't bruises, they're blue spots and I told you about them when we first came here and you made a note of it. He got the scratch from Mike's wristband and I pointed it out yesterday," I said. It was one scratch not, as the implication was, many of them. Nothing more was said. It was sickening, a betrayal of trust. I'd been uncomfortable leaving Edmund at all and knowing it had become an excuse to intimately examine him was insulting and invasive.

For those of us who couldn't get out very often or for long, boredom was a constant problem and most of the other parents watched a lot of television. A woman would come in on Tuesday afternoons to take sewing classes. Paddy, as she was called, was Irish and had been making these weekly visits since the time St Joseph's had been Catholic owned and run. I quite enjoyed them. Most of the fabric was pre-cut and we were running low on embroidery silks and material to sew. Partly out of boredom but mainly for mischief, unknown to the staff I wrote a letter to the local newspaper, explaining we were all young mothers learning life skills, such as needlework and cooking, to help us to look after our babies. I appealed to readers' generosity in asking for sewing materials to be sent in.

They printed the letter and donations came flooding in. Padded envelopes and small packets of buttons, ribbons and scraps of fabric appeared over the following days. Some came with letters from well-wishers and from the wobbly writing it was clear that the senders were elderly. As it wasn't putting our children at risk, it was taken in reasonably good spirit. The other residents thought it was hilarious but when six or so black bin liners full of fabric off-cuts were delivered, it pushed the patience of the staff. It was all very well writing to the newspaper but the large bags would have to be stored in my room. Rummaging through them at night was often quite good fun. It was a minor escape from the stress of living under the threat of losing my baby, which now seemed to be a foregone conclusion. There was little relief from this certainty. I was there to snatch a few extra months with Edmund, to take as much care of him as I could, to give Terran and Holly some memories of their half-brother.

At some point during our three-month stay, I took my bed apart and slept on the mattress. For a while, I'd been sleeping in a self-made tent under my bedroom window. It felt much safer in there. Having had much of my autonomy taken away, it was a way of claiming some independence. So was decorating the beam which supported the ceiling between the kitchenette and the main part of our room with green handprints. I'd been doing some painting with my children that day during their visit. Nobody said anything, or even knew about it. They were hidden, secret and probably only noticed when the room was decorated long after we left.

In some ways, I was free to do as I pleased but most of what I and the other residents did, or were discovered doing, was noted in the running records. If I became frustrated by the system, I couldn't show my anger or distress by crying. It was all written down and regurgitated at the monthly reviews. So were the arguments between Mike and me. Whenever the subject of Edmund's injury arose, the dormant tension climbed out and bit us.

Mike would get angry, defensive. This led to threats of, "I'll torch your house," or "I'll fight you for him," (Edmund). "Me and my mum will get him off you, you won't stand a chance. I have ways of making people believe me." Nothing else was real or tangible anymore and I was in a very vulnerable position. Mike could burn my house down and I wouldn't have been there to raise an alarm. I didn't know how to fight this, or anything else. All I wanted was to take my baby home, for him to know his family, his half-brother and sister, grandparents and the house he was born in.

My baby care was always positively commented on, the smiles and strong bond between me and Edmund was very obvious. The monthly reviews reflected this but they became darker. At the first one, we were allowed to take Edmund out each day for an unsupervised half hour. It barely gave us time to get to the park and back, but feeling fresh air on my face and wandering around the nearby shops was normalising, ordinary. After the second review, we could take Edmund out for an hour. The extra little freedom gave me a false feeling of hope.

Clearly, being given the unsupervised access showed they were all growing more confident in my parenting abilities. Whatever the weather had been like, the escape from the stifling atmosphere of the mother and baby home was a relief. Just shopping was a pleasure. Like an athlete robbed of healthy legs and given prosthetic ones, the staff expected me to be grateful. It just made me angry. We were prisoners without bars, jailed without charge and at their mercy.

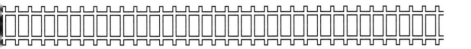

CHAPTER 7

Lifting the sash window, I climbed out on to the conservatory roof. Edmund was settling for an afternoon nap and I stood there in the fresh air, smoking a cigarette. The tree at the bottom of the garden at St Joseph's was bursting into new life. Spring was underway and the air was becoming much warmer.

We were under a lot of pressure from the Social Services. They repeated time and time again that we should be 'open and honest' with them and they could work with us, but without the admission they couldn't recommend Edmund's return home. Suggestion was made that I resented Edmund's birth, which was untrue. Mike was out of work and we had been living together for about four months when I realised I was pregnant. He seemed oblivious to the enormous responsibility of raising a child but had reluctantly tried to find a job. During my pregnancy, we had argued about it a lot. It was disappointing to realise he had little intention of financially supporting his family.

Time seemed very warped. Two years earlier, I'd been married to Derek and living in a stable but sterile and unhappy marriage. After leaving him, I spent four months homeless, started a job, bought a house and had a baby all in a very short space of time.

In spite of the upheaval and profound life changes, the tidal ebb and flow of pre- and post-pregnancy hormones, I was supposed to be able to think, make rational decisions, the *right* decisions. Right, of course, being according to the game we were playing where nobody had told us the rules. And they kept changing. They started with *if you are open and honest with us, we can work with you* to *we can't recommend Edmund to be returned to you without a confession* and *we can't recommend Edmund to be returned to you while your relationship with Mike is unstable.*

Disregarding everything, I ploughed ahead with the honest and open strategy. I knew we, or rather they, needed a confession, a guilty party, somebody to blame. It wasn't me. Had I been able to confess, I would have done it, admitted my guilt. Had they asked me to give up 20 or 30 years of my life, or cut off my legs, I would have done it – anything. So often, I implored them – our social worker, Guardian ad Litem and the staff at St Joseph's. They all nodded and smiled. The running records, which were available for residents to read on Tuesday evenings, were very positive. Yet we were both being told that Edmund wouldn't be allowed to come home without a confession, without an admission or while my relationship with Mike was unstable. So I gave up asking him, begging even, for him to admit what he had done. Once we stopped talking about it, the arguments and covert threats went away.

Apart from the times we discussed, or tried to bring up, Edmund's injury, Mike and I got on as well as we ever had. In spite of the forced separation, we remained close. Our clandestine nights together and unsupervised outings either with Edmund or on our own usually went smoothly. The memory of the first time I saw him was fixed in my mind. We were different people certainly, but I felt we were supposed to be together. We seemed to understand each other without the need for spoken language. We didn't want to lose each other. Other people, other couples, could meet their soulmates, marry and raise children in a secure and happy environment. Why not me? Why not us? Why was it always *other people*?

While we were at St Joseph's there was another hearing at the magistrates' court and Ashley came to fetch me. In other circumstances, we probably would have got on very well. As it was about a 40-minute drive, we chatted. She asked if I liked to go to nightclubs, which seemed a strange question to ask. Was she trying to build some kind of psychological profile of me? I asked her where she had studied for her degree and discovered it was the same place an old friend of mine had taught at and he was a social science lecturer. She was quite astonished when I asked if she had known him and learned, in fact, he had taught her.

It also surprised her to find out I'd been a residential social worker at a home for young offenders during the time I fell pregnant with Edmund. I lost my job because I was poor in physical restraint situations. It was like a hard slap to the face when Ashley asked if it was because I got carried away. She was trying to find out if I got violent with the young people. Exactly the opposite was true. I held back, reluctant to get involved with what I saw as provocation by the other team members. There had been an incident where one young person was literally tipped out of bed by two of the male staff. It seemed his subsequent outburst was caused directly by the goading from staff and I didn't want to get involved.

The magistrates' hearing was short. Yvonne, the forensic clinical psychologist appointed to carry out an assessment of us, was there with her report which was a favourable reflection of Mike and me as people and not what the Social Services were looking for. It was rejected because Yvonne refused to condemn us. Her remit had been to assess us and not prove culpability regarding Edmund's injury. Because Mike and I were contesting Edmund's adoption, our case would have to go to the family court. On the return journey, I didn't speak to Ashley. All I wanted to do was get back to St Joseph's and hold my baby.

Mike and I decided to get married. It would show our relationship was stable. During one of our unsupervised outings with Edmund we visited the registry office which was a five-minute walk from St Joseph's and located in a park. The surroundings were beautiful and, as spring was well under way, the weather was getting warmer. The date was set: 19th April 1994. Everyone at the mother and baby home was taken by surprise when we told them about the wedding but the residents seemed genuinely happy and excited. We invited friends, the same crowd who had regularly visited us in hospital.

Between setting the date for our wedding and the event itself, we had another review, our third and last. We had only about two weeks left at St Joseph's and our leaving date was five days after the wedding. All of the verbal feedback we had been receiving was positive, which we took to be an encouragement of our decision. Perhaps things were at a turning point. How naive of us to think that.

The assemblage of staff and social workers was, as usual, overwhelming. They had no concerns over Edmund's care but still would be unmoved from their 'no admission, no chance' stance. Not only that, Sandy, the deputy manager, pushed the knife in and twisted it. She looked across the group at me and said they had grave concerns for my mental health. I was speechless. Every time circumstance, frustration and injustices got the better of me and I'd cried in front of them or expressed any kind of anger, it had been recorded and was now being used against me.

They were equally negative about Mike. How were we supposed to suppress our feelings in such an abnormal situation? They could have been holding a death sentence in their hands in place of their reports. Edmund was lost, he was going to be adopted and I'd always known this. Another foster home was to be found, prior to the court proceedings which were made necessary because Mike and I were opposing the inevitable adoption. We were also prevented from taking Edmund out of St Joseph's on our own, even for half an hour.

I'd spent five months, which could have been a million years, taking care of him as best I could under the circumstances we were given. I'd maintained contact between my baby and his half-siblings, so they would have some memories of their baby brother. Sometimes, Holly, at her own suggestion, joined Edmund in the bath. She liked helping to wash him and they both played happily in the water, even under the watchful eye of the supervising staff. Whatever family time we created, I photographed so we could all remember the happy, healthy little boy we all loved. He had grown, in those photographs, from a few minutes' old to a baby just beginning to sit up on his own.

We got married, anyway. It was an act of desperation, a hopeless mark of unity, defiance, and love, for Edmund and each other. It was warm and sunny and I walked to the registry office with my mum and children. They were on their school Easter holiday. Edmund had to be taken by a member of staff, Patsy. Since the last review, he couldn't be taken out unsupervised at all. Mike's mum provided a colourful bouquet of anemones which I gave to Holly to hold while Mike and I made our vows. She thought they'd been given to her to keep and wouldn't give them back. She was our bridesmaid, we said, and she smiled and bounced through the whole day. My dress was bought from a local charity shop; it was short and in a black and white dog-tooth pattern. I also found a cropped pale blue denim jacket which I dyed black in the washing machine at St Joseph's. It all went nicely with some mid-calf leather boots I bought with Christmas money. I acquired a hat from somewhere, a floppy velvet heap that almost drowned my face and added cheekiness to the whole outfit. Mike had acquired a light brown suit which he wore with a new shirt and thin tie and looked really rather good.

Unbelievably, it was a very happy occasion. Our rings fitted well. Mike had done the traditional thing and measured my finger with a piece of string. His was a guess and I'd bought it on one of the visits to my solicitor. David, my brother, took the photographs. Despite the chilling undercurrent of fear, everybody was smiling and the atmosphere had a certain freedom about it. We even had a cake; made locally, it was two-tiered and white with deep yellow icing roses and edging, which we cut once back at St Joseph's. Mike and our friends took Terran and Holly to McDonald's but I didn't like to leave Edmund so stayed behind. That night was one of those where Mike pretended to leave so we were able to spend our wedding night together, locked in my room with our son sleeping in his cot by our side.

Ashley Slater came to fetch us four days later to take us to the new foster home. Edmund was six months old. I was packed and ready to leave; mine and Edmund's clothes and his toys, the belongings I'd acquired or had brought from home, were in black bin liners in the room. Unlike the first time Edmund went to foster carers, there was no hope of being reunited at a later date. This was it; thoughts of never bathing him or putting him to bed again, taking him for walks, even watching him sleeping in his own bed, overwhelmed me. Apart from the wedding, I'd spent much of the time since the review crying. They thought I was mad, anyway, so there was no point holding back my tears and nothing could have stopped them.

The Flints lived in a council house on one of the roughest estates in the borough. Brian was in his mid-50s and Kath her early 40s but both looked much older. They had a 16-year-old daughter and an eight-year-old adopted son. Their house was tidy and bland. They were both heavy smokers. It was painful to think Edmund would be exposed to such an unhealthy environment. As I'd done in the first foster home, I gave them a list of Edmund's likes, dislikes and routines. It was the first time they'd taken in a child who had come supplied with clothes, toys, nappies and food. Mrs Flint said she could tell he had been loved. I breastfed him and we both gave him a cuddle before leaving.

The care plan, which was made without our consultation, meant we would have contact with Edmund on Monday, Tuesday, Thursday and Friday at a local Family Support Centre. We could meet him at the foster home to travel with him, but as usual we'd be supervised at all times.

It was the first night I'd spent in my own bed for five months and it felt empty, hollow and cold. Mike, at the side of me, felt like a stranger.

When we turned up at the Flints' house the next morning, Edmund was in Kath's arms to meet us at the door. Like me, he had cried all night.

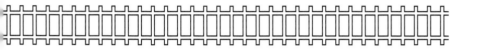

CHAPTER 8

Edmund settled down with the Flints and a new routine was quickly established. Contact was again to be monitored and supervised and on Monday, Tuesday, Thursday and Friday. I continued to breastfeed Edmund and express it for the Flints to feed him with between times but my milk soon dried up.

Mike and I would call in the morning and arrange to meet at the Flints' house. Very often, I would make the journey on my own by bus, which took about half an hour and dropped me half an hour's walk from their house. We would chat around the Flints' dining table and wait for Brian, the volunteer driver, to collect us and take us to the local Family Support Centre. The car seat Brian used was unsuitable and unsafe so I raised concerns with Ashley, who was to remain our social worker. She ignored my concerns, as she had when the first set of foster parents dressed him in the bodysuit which pulled on Edmund's toes.

Who was I to voice concerns for my baby's welfare? After all, was I not one of the potential perpetrators of the head injury which had catapulted us into this unreal situation in the first place? They no doubt would have listened and made a report on any perceived admission of guilt or intention to harm Edmund, but no mention was ever made when I expressed worries over his welfare.

As life for the past six months had revolved almost entirely around caring for Edmund and maintaining contact between him, his brother, sister and wider family, life at home was a void. Nobody else had ever bathed him, fed him and put him to bed without me being there. My job, for four days a week, was the bus journey to the Flints' house and spending time with Edmund. There were new relationships to establish, those with the support workers and staff at the Family Support Centre.

I couldn't see Terran and Holly at home. I rang Derek almost as soon as we came home from St Joseph's and Edmund was at the Flints'. He wouldn't, he said, allow me to have the children unless it was at a supervised contact centre. After so many months of them enduring visits to hospital and then the mother and baby home, it was massively important they should have some time in a real home environment – mine.

We could go to the cinema, visit the park and do ordinary things, the things we did before, but nothing was going to be the same, or even an acceptable form of nice for a very long time. It was unfair that they should have been sucked into the situation. Suddenly, after bringing up two children in the safety of a home and having many long hours on my own with them, I was an unfit mother and a potentially dangerous one at that.

Life was becoming increasingly desperate. With Edmund out of my day to day care and being back at home, there was time to reconsider and evaluate the circumstances of the past five months, perhaps longer. Not until the final review at St Joseph's did I finally realise the bleak situation we were all in. Edmund was safe, which gave me freedom to tackle the cause of his head injury and all its implications.

In spite of the Social Services' promise that cooperation, openness and honesty would go in our favour, we had been betrayed. No issues of concern were raised regarding our parenting. In fact, I'd often helped other mothers in the unit to build more positive relationships with their children by showing them how to play with and cook for them, or make toys, read and sing. Nobody had more visitors than us. Friends came and Mum and my brother David were weekly visitors, as were Terran and Holly.

We clearly had strong family and community support, had shown willingness to work with the agencies involved and had attended the psychologist's assessment appointments and magistrates' court hearings. Yet it became increasingly obvious that they, with the exception of Yvonne, were all intent on making a negative finding. No admission, no chance. That is what it all came down to.

Again, with Edmund safely and hopefully temporarily out of the way, I began pushing Mike again to admit to hurting Edmund. He wouldn't, probably couldn't. To this day, I firmly believe Mike didn't deliberately cause the injury to our baby. I'd lived with him, seen how he handled Edmund and caused him minor injuries while we were at the mother and baby home. He must have done it; I was simply unable to describe to the professionals involved what they seemed to need to know.

Lack of imagination is a key trait in people on the autistic spectrum. Everything went back to Dr Holden's *other people*. He had been the psychiatrist treating me for eating disorders in the year leading up to me leaving Derek. Most people in a similar unreal situation would have realised how to play the game; they would have known the rules nobody was telling us, which were slowly beginning to occur to me. What the Social Services had been looking for was the 'innocent' one of us to have been so repulsed by Edmund's injury that they would have taken more drastic action sooner.

My sister realised this. She had rung our social worker a day or two after Mike and I came home. I'd called into the Social Services offices to see Ashley and she told me about it. A flicker of hope was lit and instantly snuffed. Jane had, it appeared, asked why, if I hadn't caused Edmund's injury, was I still with Mike? She had also said, "I wouldn't put anything past her," and it was in Edmund's best interests to be adopted.

Ashley generously said my sister's remarks wouldn't make any difference but, judging by the satisfaction in her smile, she seemed to take pleasure in telling me. It was another devastating blow to my morale, which was threadbare enough. Jane hadn't sought to find out from me what the current circumstances were. As it had been throughout my life, the burden of troublemaker and misfit lay heavily. Most of the family had considered me mentally unstable and often told me so.

Over the months, I repeatedly asked our social worker and her line manager for advice. What should I do? What did I have to do? What did they want? Ashley seemed to get sick pleasure at witnessing my distress and I hated her for it. She was supposed to be helping. If it meant cutting off my legs, or submitting Edmund to daily health checks, I would have done it. I hadn't hurt him but couldn't prove it. There had been no marks on him to identify the perpetrator: no bites, fingerprints, witness statements, nothing. There was far more evidence to support the bond between Edmund and me, the level of care he had from me and the interaction between us. Nobody seemed interested in that. They only appeared to be interested in building a gallows-high report, tall enough to hang me from.

The only chance we had of getting Edmund home was to separate and I begged Mike to find somewhere else to live. It was the only option left. Would it work if it was temporary? Could he just go away somewhere and leave me to fight for Edmund on my own? If he could even just go away for a while, until Edmund came home and the fuss had died down, we could be together, all of us.

I was afraid of losing Mike, my soulmate, playmate, husband, who told me every day I was beautiful. I was even more afraid of losing Edmund and the wider implications that would bring such as viable contact with his siblings. Mike would be losing the security he had with me. With this threat, he again became intimidating. If we did separate, he would work against me. In a reiteration of a previous threat, he reminded me he and his mother would fight for, and win, Edmund. He had ways, he said, of making people believe him. If he couldn't have Edmund, nobody would.

Everything was unsafe, unstable, terrifying and very reminiscent of the fear I'd experienced during so much of my childhood. Edmund was in a safe place and I was glad of this. Mike refused to leave. He alternated between being loving and kind to menacing. My personal safety didn't matter. As long as I could get out of bed those four days a week when I saw Edmund, what happened in between was almost irrelevant. Mike was clinging on, we both were but something had to give, and very quickly it did.

One morning, I got up as usual and left Mike in bed. He had become sexually very demanding and I was increasingly reluctant to comply. His closeness was as compelling as ever but the need to get Edmund home was desperate. I took Mike a cup of tea and he pulled me into bed, nudging, pushing me for sex and pulled at my jeans. No, it wasn't right. He had to stop, I needed to go and see Edmund. We both had to go. It was important. Dragging myself away, I stood up and so did he. There was a bang and my cheek hurt. My soulmate, my love, had punched me. "Right, you're finished," he shouted. He was standing between me and the door, preventing escape. I pulled a pillow over my head and curled up on the bed, waiting for the beating that was sure to follow but never came.

His violence switched to an overt niceness, kind and concerned. I was in shock. In the dining room, Mike gave me a bag of frozen peas to put on my cheek, which I could see from the corner of my eye was swelling. I wanted to run but was trapped. My face was stinging but he eventually let me go and allowed me to go and see Edmund. He made his excuses for staying at home, the state of my face was probably one of them.

Maintaining the usual routine of catching the bus and walking to Kath and Brian's house, I ignored the pain and carried on as though nothing had happened. Everything was the same as ever. We had coffee, cigarettes and chatted. My cheek must have looked awful. I said nothing to them and they didn't ask. It was the same again all morning at the Family Support Centre. I played with Edmund, fed him and changed his nappy as usual, until his afternoon nap. I was in the day room, rocking his pram backwards and forwards, until he fell asleep.

Somebody walked through and I stopped her. "Would you call the police, please?" I said. "Why?" she asked. "Mike hit me," I replied, as if the lump on my face was somehow not enough. Edmund was asleep, he was safe. They took me into an office where I told them what had happened, not just that morning but so many times since we came home. Home, there was the irony. Home was supposed to be safe, a place of refuge. Edmund had been born in the same room I'd sat shaking in when Mike put the frozen peas on my face.

As soon as I'd said Mike had hit me and asked them to call the police, the practice and procedures of policy swung in and took over. Everything seemed beyond me, out of control and frightening. I was steered into action these people had training in, something they could relate to. They were enjoying the excitement. A taxi was arranged to take me to the police station after Edmund had gone back to the foster home. I refused to leave him earlier.

I was seated in an interview room and made a statement to the female police officer sent in to ask questions. The police officer, Sally, went to find cigarettes because I hadn't had one for hours. I sat in the interview room and lit one, glad of a minor distraction. My face had stopped hurting but my spirit was shredded and I wondered how far the ever lowering bar of self-esteem would go.

I was frightened.

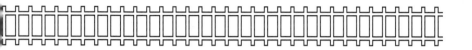

CHAPTER 9

David was there when I got home. My brother sat impassively in a chair, like our grandpa. All he would have needed to complete the picture would have been the blue haze of smoke rising from his pipe and two small girls climbing over him, putting curlers in his hair, which is what my sister and I used to do. The house was clean, tidy; Mike had clearly spent the day trying to make amends. He had cooked dinner, spaghetti bolognese. He was as frightened as me and was apologising by doing things. I'd betrayed him. The police had arrested him and taken him away. He hated the police. He spent the night in a police cell and was released after a court appearance the following morning, claiming the judge was on his side and could see how I'd been 'asking for it'. It was too confusing to cause any anger

For a while, we still shared contact with Edmund, even though Mike no longer went to the Flints' house. On most days, he would go directly to the Family Support Centre but was constantly menacing. I disliked leaving Edmund in his care, even though we were both always supervised. He would rock Edmund in his pram and make quiet threats which were hard not to respond to. Mike had quickly found a new girlfriend, who would ring him every day during his visits. I found this in bad taste and exceptionally distressing as he would go into detail about their sex life.

Eventually, it was decided that we split access, which was upsetting because it potentially meant seeing less of Edmund. I elected to have contact in the morning because if Mike failed to show, as he often did, I could stay with Edmund all afternoon and accompany him back to Brian and Kath's. This worked really well as Mike's visits were inconsistent. After a few weeks, somebody objected, which meant leaving at lunchtime regardless of whether or not Mike was there. I wasn't allowed to stay behind, even to wait for the volunteer driver with the dangerous baby seat. It was disturbing that Edmund would be there without proper supervision and be returned to the foster home on his own. Nobody listened. Who would take any notice of an unfit mother and one who may have caused Edmund's injury?

Once Mike had left, there were a few things I needed to do and one was to find a job. I'd signed on as unemployed but discovered the money to live on for food, bus fares and clothing was only £1 a week once my direct debits had been taken into account. Finding a job was imperative and it had to be in the evenings or at weekends. Losing touch with Edmund was out of the question. Without even asking, the Social Services would have simply seen it as putting career over childcare.

After attending interviews for bar work, a job in a chip shop and waking night care at a local old people's home, I applied to work as a taxi driver. My interview was on a Saturday afternoon, directly following a contact visit in Nottingham with Terran and Holly. It was a hot day and I arrived for the interview in shorts, a vest and sweating from the eight-mile cycle ride. The taxi firm was owned by Kevin and Tony. It was Tony who conducted the interview. He didn't ask to see my driving licence but I was offered a job anyway, and found out later it was because he liked my legs.

The job was welcome news and I thought it would reflect well on me with the Social Services as I elected to work three nights a week – Tuesday, Friday and Saturday – as I didn't see Edmund on Wednesdays or over the weekend and could catch up on sleep. As usual, they found something negative about it. They said I was putting myself at risk. It seemed as though everything I did was open to misinterpretation and seen in the worst light.

My job turned out to be a sanity saver. The two owners of the taxi company, Tony and Kevin, didn't care about my private life and were pleased with how hard I worked. Tuesday evenings were usually fairly quiet. As we served two towns and a handful of villages at one end of the borough, there was often a drive of quite a distance from one job to the next. Taking cassette tapes to play in the car, I would listen to music to break the quietness between customers.

During those gaps, isolation and loneliness, combined with the stress, often overwhelmed me and I would frequently sob during the drive between customers. In the darkness of the evening, customers would be greeted with a cheerful attitude and friendly chatter rather than the reality of my red eyes and tear-wet cheeks. It was good to be busy; it distracted from the inner voices telling me hope was futile, my baby was lost and I should give up because my fight was only delaying the inevitable adoption. The wider implications to consider were the effects on my older children.

In my early months as a taxi driver, I was asked out at least once or twice a night, but most of the young men who did so were reasonably accepting when they were turned down. After a while, I began to realise questions on the theme of 'Does your husband mind you doing this job?' were less out of interest in my partner's feelings and more to do with ascertaining whether or not I had one. Once I discovered their question wasn't to be taken literally, it became easy to quickly change the subject and offers of dates decreased to a less tedious level. I accepted an occasional date but was uninterested in getting involved with anyone at that time. Approaching the court date, which was set for December that year, I had a brief relationship with a young man 13 years younger than me. It was never intended to be anything other than a short fling and respite from the stress.

I was never quite sure what I would find when I got home. Once, my house was broken into and personal items were stolen. Not the usual kind of thing such as money or easy to carry appliances but selected vinyl albums I'd bought in my teens and photographs from Edmund's birth. Nobody other than Mike would steal such personal things. Who else would break into a house and remove photographs of a woman who had just given birth? The police could do nothing without evidence. He knew when I would be out of the house. Apart from the times when Edmund was ill and unable to go to the Family Support Centre, my hours away from home were regular.

On one occasion, I came home to find Mike had been round and smeared blood across the outside of the dining room windowsill. In blood, he had written one word: Why? I reported it to the police, as I did with everything that went on at home regarding Mike. The officer who took my statement asked how I knew it was Mike. "I recognise his handwriting," I said. The shock and absurdity made me laugh but it was important to have some kind of documented evidence of his threats, intimidating behaviour and menace. The desk officers at the police station began to recognise me.

It was necessary to take out an injunction against Mike, to prevent him from harassing me and keep him away from my house. I was reluctant to do this but had to be seen to be protecting not only myself but, projecting into the future, the time when Edmund would come home. It took a long while for the anxiety to subside and to distance myself from Mike. Behind all of this were questions surrounding our relationship which were unanswerable. Had he felt the same about me as I had about him or had he been playacting? It was hard not to dwell on them.

One afternoon, shortly after getting home from the Family Support Centre with my brother, two plain clothes police officers from Nottinghamshire CID knocked at the door. They showed warrant cards. I lived in Derbyshire so what were they doing here? Thinking it must have been something to do with Mike, I confirmed my name. "We are investigating the disappearance of a baby from Queen's Medical Centre in Nottingham," they said. I was stunned. What did it have to do with me?

My details had been passed on to them. "Who gave you my name and address?" I asked. Apparently, I fitted the psychological profile. They were questioning any woman who had lost a baby in some way. My name, along with many others', could have been on many lists. As it wasn't the kind of conversation to conduct on a doorstep, I invited them inside. It was very clear there was no way the kidnapping could have had anything to do with me. I'd been at the Family Support Centre with my brother until lunchtime on the day the baby was taken and had had an interview for a job in an old people's home later on.

I was helpful and polite. Yes, of course I'd heard about the four-hour-old baby's abduction, just the same as everyone else in the country had. Why would I steal somebody else's baby? I was busy with my own. The tiny newborn baby girl had been taken from her father's arms by the abductor, who had posed as a health worker and simply walked out of the hospital with her. No doubt they would also want to look around my house. They declined the invitation.

The story was headline news in the local paper and there was nationwide media coverage every day until after the little girl was found. Three people were arrested and Baby A was reunited with her parents over two weeks later. Of course, the police had to follow up every name given to them but this was just another blemish on the ugly face of the situation. More than once, it had crossed my mind to kidnap my own son but thoughts like that were fleeting. It wouldn't have been sustainable and would have made the situation a whole lot worse, if that was possible.

Seeing other people with their young children was painful and going out was difficult. Their lives were a world away from mine. Ordinary, stable, taking for granted the school run, broken nights, toddler groups and meeting their friends and families. I felt as though everyone could literally see labels stuck all over me like nasty little Post-it notes, each one a mud splat bearing nasty words: baby killer, baby snatcher, bad mother, useless, evil, failure, dangerous, selfish, rotten. I felt dirty, as though I'd been turned into a subhuman life form.

More than ever, it was as though the world was a series of events happening through a one-way plate glass window. Other autistic people have described life in similar ways. We can see and hear the world but interacting with it was painful, impossible or both. I used to think I was invisible and having anyone talk to me was a shock.

During this time, we were referred for more psychological assessments. Yvonne, who we had seen together while at St Joseph's, had produced a report which was discredited in the magistrates' court. She had had little time to prepare and had been unclear on what she was being asked to do. Seeking clarification from the Guardian ad Litem, she was instructed not to make a finding on the perpetrator, which she nevertheless did and it wasn't the one anyone had wanted to hear.

On the balance of probabilities, Yvonne had concluded that Mike was the person more likely to have injured Edmund. Because of this, her evidence had gone down badly and another clinical psychologist was instructed to make a new report. This meant travelling to Leicester to see Anna, who worked at a secure centre in the city's mental hospital. If it meant walking, it was important to attend all three of the hour-long sessions. Unknown to me there was a railway workers' strike on the day of the first appointment. No trains were running.

There was no alternative, short of the walk option, but to catch the bus, which would make me late. It was a five-minute walk from the railway station and I'd no idea what time the buses to Leicester ran. Incredibly, there wasn't too long to wait, which gave me time to ring Anna to warn her of my delay. The urgency was suffocating. I needed to be there. Surely my effort would demonstrate my commitment? Other people again; *other people* may have acted differently. Maybe they would have rung to rearrange the appointment, or realised there was a rail strike, or phoned a friend to give them a lift. But I wasn't *other people*. My son's future depended upon the impression I made and I needed to be there, regardless. Anna only saw me for half an hour but we made other appointments, which I kept.

At the end of the third appointment with Anna, which had, I felt, gone extremely well, she said, "I hope it all goes well for you." It was a relief. Having now separated from Mike, finding a job and keeping every possible appointment, it gave me hope. A copy of her report was sent to my solicitor and was devastating. In spite of her encouraging words, Anna had little to say which was positive. As with everyone else, she had been paid to make a negative finding. She hadn't mentioned the effort it had taken to keep the appointments, especially the first one. Anna said she had seen me for a total of three hours, which was untrue. Because of my late arrival owing to the train strike, she had actually only seen me for two and a half hours.

Much was said about my apparent mood swings and history of depression. At times, I'd been tearful because of the desperation of the situation and I'd spoken passionately about my hopes and fears. Still taking the advice given by the Social Services literally, I'd spoken with transparent honesty, especially regarding my childhood, my father's alcoholism, the fear of violence at home, and the report had succeeded in putting a dark spin on everything. She had outlined her intention to focus her risk assessment on me, as Edmund's mother, as Mike hadn't attended any of his appointments. He was ascribed a short paragraph which mentioned his early childhood abuse and psychiatric history. From the reports she'd been given, Anna concluded that Mike posed a considerable risk to Edmund but that I couldn't be discounted from either causing or colluding in our baby's injury.

I sat in Fay's tiny office and cried. I said, "Why don't I just give up and let them take him? What chance do I stand of ever getting Edmund home?" She said, "Don't give up, never give up." Her words were strengthening and have carried me over the years from one difficult situation to another. Don't give up, never give up. The fight continued – for myself, for Edmund and for Terran and Holly. Losing Edmund would have given Derek more reason to refuse unsupervised contact with the older children.

I began to see a therapist at the Child and Adolescent Mental Health service (CAMHs) in Nottingham. He was Spanish and his accent made him hard to understand but I felt he may be able to write a favourable report. My appointments all had to be on Wednesdays so as not to interfere with seeing Edmund, but I trusted him as he hadn't been commissioned by the Social Services and would, therefore, be more honest and less damning in his appraisal. In the end, he wasn't called to write anything but he did offer a flickering candle of hope. He was the first person to say there was, in fact, a chance Edmund could be returned home. Maybe he was being naive, or I was, but hope was needed and this was, for once, something positive. Even though it was a small chance, I set myself the task of making it bigger. Once it became bigger, I wanted it bigger still. It had to be huge.

I saw a King Charles spaniel advertised for sale in a pet shop window and decided home was too quiet so bought him. He became a distraction from the anxiety I experienced when I was at home alone.

I also started to dance.

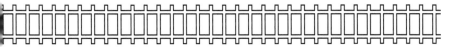

CHAPTER 10

Strangely, it was Mike who first told me about a Christian 'rave' night started by some of its younger members. It was set out in the church hall rather than the church itself and was styled on a contemporary nightclub. They used theatre lighting, strobes, rotating spotlights and had images projected on to huge screens. Instead of hymns and songs, they had a mixing desk at the back and played techno music. They met on the first Sunday in the month and my first time there was a disaster: Mike was there, smirking, as though expecting me. I left immediately. Thinking he was stalking me, I went straight to the local police station and reported him. There was nothing they could do so I went home, afraid he might come to the house.

When I did eventually go, it was outstanding. The nightclub-style setting was buzzing and the hall was packed with people enjoying the contemporary dance music which could be heard from the street. Among the noise, moving lights and images, I found a voice. Making my way to the front, I threw myself into the pulsing electric techno beat. It was like flying in space, twirling, stamping, hopping, punching and spinning among the stars which were too many to count. It was like touching the fingers of angels. I was alive. All the frustration, anger, rage and restraint the months of constant scrutiny had brought were lost for a while. Nobody was watching me, writing down everything I said or did. My body spoke everything which was wordless. I danced away the hurt, the guilt, the shame of my situation. I was a bird, flying my way to freedom.

At home, I would dance. In the evenings, I closed the curtains, shutting out the painful world, put on music and expended the energy of a newly released prisoner. It was a wonderful freedom, relaxing, invigorating and life giving. I bought new music. It was strengthening my soul and I began to sleep better. Not only that, the friendships I built lasted for many years, carrying me across the difficult months to follow and long afterwards. Two of the founders were brothers. Gavin was a set designer and Simon was a sound and light technician. Their mother, Maureen, was one the warmest people I had ever met. Her support, solid and unspoken, was practical and enduring. These people were not duplicitous but took me as I was – a real person, vulnerable, afraid and human. They were distractions on bad days and supportive on better ones. In spite of everything, I was building a new life.

I made friends with someone I met one morning at the bus stop while on my way to spend the day with Edmund. The woman, Pascale, was French and a glass artist who worked at a studio in the town. She was setting up evening classes where she worked and I joined them. Doing something practical and creative was therapeutic and the result, a coloured glass panel, looked really good. Learning how to hold and use the glass cutter, shape the lead and put it together was interesting. Pascale had made the patterns, which looked like the outlines of unfinished pictures from a children's colouring book, herself. We often went for a drink afterwards and became very close friends for a couple of years, occasionally even going out together on other evenings. It was very good to know people outside my day to day situation and not to have them recoil from me because of my circumstances. They all knew about my situation and the baby I could only talk about, the one they were unlikely to ever meet.

All of the assessments had been done. Nobody at the Family Support Centre was to be asked to write a report or evaluate either my parenting or Mike's. They were merely there to facilitate our supervised contact with Edmund prior to the court hearing. As they'd been instructed in the magistrates' court hearing, the Social Services were not allowed to pre-empt the judge's recommendation. It was something to object to yet accept. I couldn't even change my baby's nappy unless somebody was watching but the friendliness of the staff made a difference; without this, the whole process would have been so much more humiliating, although I never understood why anyone would think I could have hurt my own baby when my children, all of them, were precious.

Derek had two children from his first marriage and had a vasectomy after the second one was born. He had it reversed some months after we got married and I fell pregnant reasonably easily. It was two and half years before I felt ready to add to the family but this time we were less lucky, I didn't conceive. As had been a problem for a number of years, my menstrual cycle was erratic. I could go eight or ten weeks between periods and often felt ill the whole time. Friends met, married and had children of their own. Every night, after reading his bedtime story, Terran and I had prayed for a baby sister.

Eventually, after two years of trying, disappointment and hurt, we were told we could have no more children. Scar tissue from the vasectomy reversal operation had built up, leaving Derek effectively sterile. It was heartbreaking. The drive home from the hospital on the day we were given the news is a journey tattooed in my memory. I can still feel the cold December sunshine on my face and see the horizon line sink as our car descended the ramps in the multi-storey car park.

Most couples in similar situations would empathise; they know how life is lived month by month, with hope building up and then fading into another disappointment. Career changes and long-term plans are put on hold because surely this month will be a lucky one. My mother-in-law said we should be grateful for Terran, which we were, but our choice had been taken away. Deciding to have one child was quite different from being told we could have no more. I cried for weeks. The pain seemed endless. At any small frustration or at the remotest stress, I would burst into tears, paralysed with grief. Andy, my driving instructor, was a very patient man and would simply wait for me to stop crying before carrying on with the lesson. It must have added to his own hurt as his wife had suffered from many miscarriages, even quite late into her pregnancy.

I began to explore the possibility of doing other things, perhaps by returning to education, gaining some qualifications and getting a better job, one with more prospects. Terran was to start school the following Easter, the weather was getting warmer and a little hope returned to our lives. We looked at adopting a child and started to attend introductory talks at the local Social Services offices and sat in a group with other parents whose interest, like ours, had been inspired by a series on television called *Find Me a Family*. We had turned down the offer of fertilisation by donor as we didn't think it was right for us, but this television programme showed children, either individual or in sibling groups, looking for 'forever families'.

I went to the doctor because I was tired and angry with my erratic menstrual cycle and wondered if something could be done. It annoyed me when he questioned me after I'd said there was no possibility of being pregnant. "Look in my notes," I said. He did but still insisted I take a urine sample down the following week and a week after that he told me it was positive. I was ten weeks pregnant. Holly was born almost a year after we were given no chance. Terran had the baby sister we had prayed so hard for.

I was 'open' and 'honest' with the Social Services. They wanted to build up a picture of me. They knew about my previous fertility issues. How could they then think it at all possible that I would suddenly become a virtual child killer? It was a different relationship; they had counter arguments for everything. The picture they wanted to build, it seemed, would be one of Medea, the ancient Greek witch who killed her own children. That I'd left my children with their father when our marriage broke down was used in their very negative portrayal of my parenting.

Society is very biased against mothers who leave the marital home just as much as it is in failing to recognise the value of fathers in their children's care. It so often seems that a departing man is 'walking out on his wife and kids' whereas a mother is seen as abandoning her children. Eighteen months earlier, when I left, many people asked why I either didn't take the children with me or force Derek to leave. I valued my by then ex-husband as a caring and responsible father and saw no reason to cause more difficulties for our children than absolutely necessary.

Interwoven in all of this were my unrecognised autism and the difficulties people on the autistic spectrum have when coping with change. That aspect was a familiar friend. From childhood, I experienced many problems in this area. When my own children were born, I would make a point of preparing them for change and get them actively involved, which, without knowing it, was an autism sympathetic approach. As a result, my children always handled changes a great deal better than I ever could have done because they were allowed to.

The Social Services were silent when asked why the positives regarding my childcare abilities and the bond between me and Edmund hadn't been taken into account. It seemed they were simply looking for excuses, reasons or whatever else they may have called them to remove Edmund permanently from my care. Ashley remained our social worker throughout the 11-month wait for the court hearing and would call in at the centre to see us occasionally. Outwardly, she was friendly but maintained her insistence that I was making things harder for Edmund by delaying the inevitable adoption. Their reports of him 'presenting as a white British baby' were troubling. It was much easier, she told me, for babies to adapt the younger they were adopted yet, if he were adopted, his new family wouldn't know he was mixed race and Edmund would have lost an important part of his heritage.

I knew 'white British babies' for adoption were in short supply. On many occasions, I asked her if she had already identified a 'nice British couple' for Edmund. Ashley denied it but I'd already been through too many months of being lied to and deceived to believe her. I was sick of asking, "What do I have to do? What do you want from me? Shall I cut off my legs? I will bring him, every day, to be examined but let me, please let me just take my baby home." She would look at me, blankly, blindly. Inside, I was screaming. That they, Ashley and Anne, might think I could present a wonderfully healthy cared for and loved baby one day and his dead body the next was numbing.

Even Edmund too, it seemed, thought me a danger to live with as his Guardian ad Litem proposed adoption. As he was there to speak for Edmund, it was deemed to be his opinion. It seemed strange that Edmund himself was seeking a new family; also, bizarrely, the Guardian didn't seem to be independent at all. There was a bias and it was weighted heavily against the family. His solicitor, appointed by Derbyshire County Council, was yet another person representing 'Edmund's best interests'. We were going to court, my mum, brother, me and Yvonne, a tiny army against a well-oiled machine which was poised, experienced, fully armed and ready to play their deadly game. The rest of us had to pick up the rules as we went along. Every turn was a blind bend.

Back at home, I played music and danced.

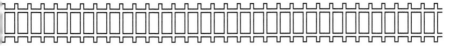

CHAPTER 11

Rowena, my barrister, had told me the Social Services on the whole were very nervous following the murder of three-year-old Leanne White in neighbouring Nottinghamshire the year before Edmund was born. She was beaten to death by her stepfather, with her mother being complicit by failing to protect her daughter. At her inquest, she was found to have 107 external injuries. It made national news and the full horror of Leanne's death was widely reported in the media. This was something which would have been, Rowena told me, in the minds of Derbyshire Social Services.

The case cast its clammy fingers over the child protection system and the authorities became uber vigilant. It was, as it too often has been, a case of shutting the metaphoric gate after the horse has bolted. Public shock demanded action to prevent another young life being taken at the hands of their carers. Yet they tragically do; children have continued to be abused and ultimately die through the systematic failure of those who should know better. In every reported case of children dying at the hands of those who supposedly rock the cradle, there is an invariable history of neglect and abuse. There was none of this in our case. There was no horse to bolt yet I found myself fenced into a rocky corral.

Edmund's first birthday fell on the Tuesday of the school half-term break which made it easy to arrange for Terran and Holly to join us for the day. His first and maybe the only one we would be able to celebrate with him. It had to be special. Instead of catching the bus to the Flints' house that morning, I booked a taxi to take me there. Part of me wanted to prove to the world that I had a baby, even if it was just one of the drivers I worked with. Unlike other parents, nobody saw me leave the house with him, smilingly asking how he was and commenting on how fast he was growing. We never sat waiting to see the health visitor or chatted in the supermarket with other mothers, our children in the trolley seats.

I'd bought a large box of building bricks which was too large to carry and the clown cake I made the day before may not have survived the long walk from the bus. Daniel, Edmund's eight-year-old foster brother helped him to open the presents. Both boys were still in pyjamas and there was little time to play, but Daniel carried on playing with the bricks while I got Edmund ready to go out. Joy mixed with intense grief. The happiness of him being alive was wonderful but the awareness it could be the first and last birthday we would celebrate with him for many years was a strong undercurrent.

If he ever wanted to trace his birth family once he reached 18, maybe we would have lost time to catch up with, but what would he be told as he grew up? Would the story be that his mummy and daddy had hurt him? Would we be allowed to make a memory box with an album of photographs and letters to give him, explaining my side of the story or fight to keep him and tell him of the intense love I had for him? I often wondered what his adoptive family would be told about my son's background. I could only suppose they would have been given a story which would reinforce their assumption that their new child had somehow been saved from an awful home and baby killer mother.

He had to have the best possible birthday, something Terran and Holly would remember. I arranged for them to join us for the day at the Family Support Centre. It wasn't home and we should have been out on an adventure somewhere but we had grown used to making the best of the time we spent together. It was important to make the day as special as possible. The three children had rarely met as a family group after we left St Joseph's five months earlier. They were innocently unaware of the reality of the situation we were in and as Edmund had been living in an unnatural environment for almost all his life, they accepted the strange circumstances completely.

We had a room at the Family Support Centre to ourselves and Terran and Holly arrived to find me standing on a chair, putting birthday banners around the walls. A fish on a bicycle would have looked more at home than those banners, which looked lost against a background of other children's paintings. I was, by now, quite used to parenting under close supervision, being monitored and watched, and we all simply got on with it, paying little attention to whoever was with us. On this day, it was Tracey, who worked as a residential social worker in a children's home and came in once a week to enable Edmund to have a room on his own, away from the other children. She stayed all day, monitoring Mike's access in the afternoon.

It was still very similar to being visited in prison as we were still not free to go out on our own, but the environment was very much better than the few weeks we had seen each other at the children's home six months earlier. Tracey was in the early stages of pregnancy herself so may have enjoyed the lack of physical demands her days with us involved. We got on as well as circumstances allowed and it was lucky for us that Edmund had his birthday on the same day that Tracey was there. Sometimes we all went out together, to break the monotony of the institutionalised environment, although the weather was now becoming autumnally damp and dreary. I tried to treat her as a friend but was very aware that, in spite of no longer having my parenting monitored, she too was in the employment of the Social Services and only had my limited trust.

Having such large gaps in the ages of my children (there were over ten years between my sons) should have made occupying them quite hard, especially with a daughter in the middle. It was fortunate they were not spoiled, petulant children and were happy with straightforward pastimes. Terran chalked a fish picture on the drawing easel. Once busy, he was difficult to distract but I learned early on in his life that he needed to focus on something because he was difficult to live with when bored.

I never knew what to expect from parenthood. With Terran, it was very obvious from birth he had a unique character as independent from me as his hands and feet were. As the first grandchild on my side of the family, I had no nephews or nieces to learn from and few of my friends had children at that time. Mothers are usually a good source of advice and guidance but mine was so full of old wives' tales it was difficult to separate sound knowledge from utter nonsense. Terran was born five days before my 22nd birthday, during an exceptionally hot summer, and we learned from each other. He was a frustrated baby, always trying to do things beyond his physical abilities and would rarely attempt anything new unless he had first worked out how to do it. His brain gave out almost mechanical clicks and whirrs as he processed information because, at least to me, it was very obvious what he was trying to achieve.

Moving between developmental stages was accompanied by fury from trying to grasp an out of reach toy to rolling over. I would help him by holding objects away from him but close enough to grab so the final effort was his. It was the same when he learned to roll from his back to his tummy. He got halfway but couldn't quite manage the final turn. He would scream with rage. A supportive hand to his back enabled him to complete the task. This kept him happy for a number of weeks until he managed on his own but again became angry at being unable to crawl. He achieved this at four months by pulling himself on to his hands and knees and rocking to and fro until he flipped forwards. He didn't begin walking independently until 14 months as he was quite content to use the furniture to move around.

The frustrated baby grew into a similarly attributed toddler who was quite happy when busy and rarely demanded my attention. He could be given a task and absorb himself in it for a remarkable length of time but was dreadful when he had nothing to focus on. I took to reading to him almost from birth, just to keep his mind occupied. We joined the library and Terran would choose his own books as soon as he could walk. I would take him out of his pushchair and ask which books he would like. It was like winding the key in the back of a clockwork robot because he always knew where to find his latest favourite genre.

Without me being at all aware of autism at the time, Terran was displaying obvious traits of the condition. He went through very clear and distinct areas of interest as he grew up. In no particular order, he travelled through phases of spiders and snakes, farming and farm machinery, space travel, reptiles, dinosaurs and hand tools. As he passed through each special interest, the growing boy would absorb an incredible amount of facts in his chosen subject; for instance, he could recite all kind of dates and names regarding early space travel and the Moon landings in the late 1960s and early 1970s.

While he was unable to read, I learned too, as it was usually me who would look at the books with him. Children's non-fiction books are fantastic in the way they present information. They generally hold enough facts to educate, have straightforward diagrams and illustrations, and do not bog the reader down with too much technical information. My son's special interests were similar to his physical development in as much as he closed the chapter and never looked back once he had achieved everything he needed from it. It was as though he was saying 'done that what next?'

His self-containment extended to his feelings. Terran rarely said he was bored or felt ill or any of the things other children would normally do. His behaviour was the clearest indication that something was different. He would express boredom through using moderately challenging behaviour. He was unconcerned about it being Edmund's birthday and showed little interest in me but that was typical. If he was busy, he was happy. This probably made it much easier to entertain the three children.

Holly was very much a butterfly, flitting between activities: drawing, playing with the Support Centre toys or talking to Edmund. Over the months, she often asked when Edmund was going home or when they could go to my house. I kept it simple and told her I would have to go and see a man called a judge. Some people wanted Edmund to have a new mummy because he got hurt and nobody knew how it happened but the judge would decide where Edmund was going to live.

Each child had something to do and all were contented. Terran was his own universe, Holly flitted; Edmund was played with, carried and followed around. At the time, he was obsessed with turning on taps and would crawl to the bathroom, where he could reach the tiny sinks. That was how his first birthday was, until shortly after lunch and time to leave him there for Mike to take over until Edmund went 'home'.

Memories of the day were archived, stored in a freshly painted box in my mind somewhere. It was a cold damp day so I stepped outside the Family Support Centre to be met by drizzle, gloom and Mike, who had shown up with gifts of his own. Leaving my baby there was painful as there was still so much of the day left. It would have been so nice to have celebrated at home, with friends and their children. Something ordinary; I never thought about normal because that, for us, was normal. It was like walking through the door of an inverted Tardis where the world inside was small and the outside vast and endless. As I walked up the path to the road, my pace gathered speed. It was still Tuesday and I needed to go to work, to live, to stay alive.

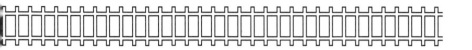

CHAPTER 12

The court date was a few days away and I was sick with nerves. Life had an established routine and perverse security. It had fallen into a predictable pattern: visiting Edmund, the days in the Family Support Centre, seeing my other children and work. The change which had to happen was anticipated with equal amounts of dread and welcome. Life was static and the only way to move it on was to go through with the proceedings unless, of course, either I or the authorities stepped out of the ring and stopped the fight. That was never going to be an option either side would take.

I'd never seen inside a courtroom of that kind, only a magistrates' court. My barrister Rowena and solicitor Fay tried to prepare me. As it was a family court and because nobody had been charged with an offence, it was called a hearing rather than a trial. There would be no jury, just one judge who, like the barristers, would be in a suit and not the black gown and wig of television courtroom dramas. Of course, somebody was on trial but nobody had been charged with any offence. I was on trial and so was my family. So was Yvonne, whose earlier report in the magistrates' court was rejected. We had to prove we could support and raise a small child, that my troubled background was going to stay where it belonged, in the past, and not follow me into the future.

A few days before the start of the hearing, I had a dream. I was in court, in the witness box, facing the right side of the judge, who looked remote, distant, behind his light wood bench. Below him, to the front, was a table. Nobody sat there. The courtroom was empty. The rows of benches, which looked like church pews, were below to my right. Beyond those were layered seats, similar to those in theatres or cinemas. I cast my eyes around the bright, modern-looking furniture and high-windowed walls, taking in everything until I'd gazed a full circle back to the judge, who was holding my toddler son on his lap.

Edmund was playing with something on the desk in front of him, ignoring me. The judge was a slightly built man with dark hair. I watched him for one of those short times which seem to last for hours until he looked at me and spoke. "You can take your baby home," he said. From deep within my soul there was a long shrill scream, like the whine of a life-support machine turned off. I woke with three words, *the third day, the third day*, running through my mind; they rattled around in the echoing hollow of an empty room somewhere in another life, on another planet.

I shared the dream and those words with my friends on the Sunday evening, which was a service night. I'd danced like Satan's best friend or Nero's favourite slave jumping through flames in the fire of impending hell as Rome burned to ashes to the sound of his fiddle playing.

Mum had taken the week off work and my brother, who had no job to take leave from, came with us to the county court where the hearing was being held. It was December 5th, one year and one day since Ed was admitted to hospital. The waiting area was a cold corridor, as cheerless as a funeral parlour, and opened directly on to the street outside. It must have been very cold for those like my family who had to keep their vigil there for the week. As Edmund's parents, Mike and I could sit in the courtroom although no one knew whether or not he would be there. He had elected not to give evidence. He came sweeping in and looking arrogant as he strode through the large double doors wearing a long black leather coat I'd never seen before. Liz, his mum, followed slowly behind him.

Uncomfortable silence hung over everyone. The only noise was the quiet click of Mum's knitting needles, which ticked away in a clockwork rhythm. Time was running out. Everybody seemed to be someone else's enemy where once we had been family.

David looked smart; his trousers and dark jacket, clean complexion and poise held a quiet confidence. My brother had always been someone to keep his feelings to himself and chose his words carefully. He was very much like our paternal grandfather who said little but thought a lot, so when he had something to say, which was always in a considered and direct way, it mattered. Like Mum, he had been a regular visitor to the hospital, St Joseph's and the Family Support Centre and had a strong bond with his nephew. Over and above the relationships he had with my other children, his relationship with Edmund, along with his deeply held sense of justice, gave him a humane yet solid air.

It was time; we were all called into the courtroom. I faltered for just a moment in the doorway. Leaving my family to wait with Sandy from St Joseph's and Val from the Family Support Centre, I went in. Lost for breath, the court looked exactly as it had in my dream. I was seated at the end of a bench directly behind Rowena and the other legal representatives, although Fay was on my right with Margaret, her secretary, between me and Ashley, who sat next to Anne O'Connor, her manager. They were the only two who looked remotely comfortable, smiling and whispering to each other like two giggling girls at a family wedding.

Mike sat at the back, on the public seats, rather than with his solicitor. Whilst he had declined to give any evidence himself, he was supporting the motion to have Edmund placed for adoption. It was impossible to guess why he was even present; it could have been to unsettle me or even silently influence the judge by his arrogant attitude and smug air. I almost expected him to start whistling, something he used to do casually when he had upset me in the far too recent past. He didn't use any of the seats but elevated himself by perching on a seat back, his feet resting on the back of the seat in front. In his large black leather coat, he looked like a perched raven ready to swoop.

Silence fell as we all stood when the judge entered. Circuit Judge David Browning had on a light grey suit. It was clear his silver hair had once been dark and he looked just as the judge had in my dream. He could have had Ed on his lap because the fate and future of my son would rest on his decision alone. Looking around at the uncanny similarities between my dream and the surreal picture in front of me, it could have been said that Edmund's fate had been decided upon many years ago. If only it could be true.

I'd taken paper and a pen and throughout the days of the hearing would frequently write down questions to pass forward for Rowena to ask the witness. It was quite disturbing to see the number of people called by the Social Services to give evidence and something I hadn't anticipated. Brian Flint, Edmund's foster father, was there. He still wore the teddy boy hairstyle of his youth and most people would have accurately guessed he was a big Elvis Presley fan. More used to seeing him in jeans and an open-necked shirt, he looked uncomfortable in the suit he wore yet he still carried an air of down to earth honesty about him.

Brian was questioned on how Mike and I had presented to him as Edmund's parents and had he ever had any concerns for the child's welfare. He hadn't. His time in the witness box was brief. Val, for the Family Support Centre, had a more professional look. In her late 40s and with the husky voice of a heavy smoker, I smiled as she put on her best speaking voice, which did little to disguise her strong local accent. In common with Brian, she had nothing negative to say concerning the care given to Edmund by either of his parents. They'd both spoken favourably yet neutrally of us. Both Val and Mr Flint were questioned on whether or not they considered the relationship between Mike and me to be over and it became increasingly obvious over the rest of the week that much importance was being placed on this.

Although no formal reports or assessments had been conducted during our time at the Family Support Centre, Tracey had been called as a witness. She had spent so much one to one time supervising the contact between Edmund and me, and also with Mike in the afternoons, she was ideally positioned to voice her observations. She was excused. Owing to her pregnancy, she was unwell. I saw her again ten years later in a local supermarket and she brought up her non-appearance at the hearing. She had been ill, she admitted, but the main reason was that she disagreed with the proceedings and didn't believe I'd hurt my baby and strongly suspected that no one else at the time did either. It served to confirm my suspicions that the system, without an admission of guilt, was loaded against me – not only me but my son's right to a family life. If the Human Rights Act had been in place at the time the bias may not have been weighted so strongly in favour of the system.

Tim Jaspan and Terence Stephenson, neither of whom we had seen since we left hospital, were called and questioned at length by the different solicitors representing the Social Services, Edmund, the Guardian ad Litem and Mike about the factual information regarding Edmund's injury. Especially from the medical perspective, it was traumatic to hear the details over a year on and in the court setting. The medical professionals refuted the notion that the injury could have happened accidentally. Dr Jaspan said the kind of force used to cause such a head trauma would have been like the impact of throwing the child through a car window at 70 miles an hour. It had never occurred to me before I heard my barrister cross-examining him that surely, if this was the case, there would have been other injuries to the baby such as bruising to his body or a broken neck.

Some years later, I did some research of my own and discovered that new evidence regarding infantile head injuries showed they took much less of an impact than once thought. Hearing such a blatantly obvious question asked in that formal setting was powerful. As the consultant paediatrician, Dr Stephenson had little personal contact with the children on the wards himself, or their parents, but he had not heard anything negative regarding my care of Edmund. Rowena's questions were beginning to make me look more of a human being and less of a potential threat to my baby.

When Anna Morris, who had undertaken the three sessions at the Leicester psychiatric hospital, was questioned, it seemed to be very clear she had been paid very well to make a negative finding against me, the one for which Yvonne had been dismissed and discredited for refusing to do. I looked at her with a sense of betrayal, remembering how well we had seemed to get on, how open I'd been, and her parting words on my last visit when she said, "I hope it all goes well for you." How unwittingly had I fallen, time after time, into believing the lie that being open and honest with them would go well for me?

Keeping an outward peace but inwardly writhing in disgust, my contempt at Sandy seethed. Throughout her evidence, she never once lifted her face to look at the judge. All David Browning would have seen of her was the top of her head and her short ginger hair.

Red-faced throughout, she mumbled her answers to her hands, which were pressed one on top of the other against the surface of the witness box. Rowena asked her why she had made note of a remark I made to Edmund in the kitchen at St Joseph's. "Why did you note in the daily records that my client said 'Oh Ed, you are a pain sometimes'?" Sandy's face grew increasingly scarlet. "I was trying to make a finding," she answered. "So you think a comment like that, made by my client, would indicate her as the perpetrator of Edmund's injury?" Rowena pressed in. "No," Sandy whispered. It wasn't worth the paper to pass forward a question for Rowena to ask. Had I done so, it would have been for her to point out the many occasions Sandy had visited my house during my first marriage when Terran was a toddler, and had she perceived any threat there?

The first two days were encouraging but there was a sickening punctuation when Ashley entered court on the second day with medical records for both Mike and me. She took them into a side room and threw them on to the table. She, Anne and Paul were like starving ravens over roadkill, picking the flesh from crushed bones. They would see and use our mental health histories and maximise the potential danger to such a small child his parents posed. As Mike was making no application for Edmund, the thrust of attention fell solely on my medical history.

The arguments of the social worker and Guardian ad Litem had been weakened by Rowena's questions. Before the court was adjourned at the end of the day, Tuesday afternoon, I knew I would be in the witness box the following morning. Remembering the words which woke me from my earlier dream, the third day was indeed going to be significant. Using the wall-mounted telephone in the corridor at the court, I rang the first person on the church prayer chain to pass on the news of the day's proceedings for the second time. This person would then call the next person on the list and so on until everyone knew and they could all pray. I would need those prayers.

Outside was cold and darkness was falling. I had to go to work. My brother sat in the back of Mum's car and we headed out of town. Having taken my work clothes with me, I changed out of my smart skirt, blouse and neat blue shoes into my work clothes as we drove. Ready for the night shift and much in need of something which felt normal, it would be one o'clock in the morning before I saw my house again.

My employers at the taxi firm knew about the childcare proceedings but I rarely discussed them. If I talked about it at all, which I frequently did, it was with friends, family or those who knew Edmund. To anyone who had never met him he was something of a mythological creature and at times it felt as though he was part of a fantasy world, not really there at all. He and everything surrounding him was an alter world, separate from the real one, the one in which I lived and worked. I wanted people to meet him, to know him, so I could remind them after his adoption that I did have a baby once, and he was beautiful. Showing photographs of him covered in dinner, riding a little tricycle around the yard at the Family Support Centre or sitting in a swing was a poor substitute for meeting friends in the park.

We had traversed an entire year under the scrutiny of one place or another, beneath the smiling veneer of mutinous faces. Bringing him into my waking world would have convinced me that he was an actual living baby who was part of my life. He could have been the treasure from my childhood dream, consigned forever to stay in my sleeping hours, never to cross into human existence, one which others could touch and experience. I couldn't hold him and bring him back any more than I could have stuffed discovered treasure in my dreams under my pillow to cherish on waking. That is, essentially, what travelling by train is, a drift from one place to another, and we are all spectators through the window where one life passes through another.

That night I had another dream. Roman soldiers, too many to count and in bright red uniforms, plumed helmets and dazzlingly bright breastplates entered the court waiting room. Carrying spears and with swords at their sides, they moved slowly and quietly in two lines. On either side of the corridor, in two rows, they placed their spears on the floor behind them, underneath the benches they silently sat down on. There was going to be no fighting from these men. Instead, in unison and still without a word passing between them, they bowed their heads and prayed. Angels, I thought, angels were watching over us.

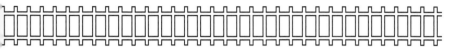

CHAPTER 13

It was Wednesday, the third day and my turn in the witness box. My earlier feeling had proved accurate which, combined with the dreams, was eerie but strangely comforting, creating a creeping notion that much of this was decided by forces which operated outside earthly time and space. One can question the existence of God, but many events, even before Edmund was born, went beyond simple human assumptions or expectation.

One of these occurred just after Holly was born, the first time I drove her anywhere on my own after her birth. She was about ten days old. I parked on our driveway and got out of the driver's seat. As I opened the rear passenger door to take my new baby daughter out, a voice spoke into my soul so clearly it could even have been audible. It said, "You'll have another baby and it'll be a boy." There was no indication he was going to have a different father, it would be another life or that he would be taken away from me. Indeed, it was as though the damp, depressing drizzle in the air was indicative of a greater battle, one conducted outside time, space or this planet.

As had been the case with the first two days, I wore a different outfit and this one, the smartest of all, had been saved for the occasion.

It was a calf-length dress in navy blue and decorated with small white triangles. Over it I wore a long cardigan matching the dress in colour. My shoes, which I'd worn with every other outfit, were also navy blue, flat and fastened with small round buttons. It wasn't hard to be composed as fear had frozen me.

Declining the oath, I asked to make an affirmation instead. As instructed, I answered each question carefully, looking at the judge rather than the questioner. It was helpful advice as Mike was smirking from his perch at the back of the court. If he could have, he looked as though he would have whistled in derision, the way he used to when we argued and I cried tears of anger. He had been like that at the Family Support Centre, whispering threats and taunts out of earshot of anyone else, so when I exploded at him it reflected badly on me, especially when he remained calm and outwardly cooperative towards staff.

My life and that of my children depended on the impression I made. Peace drew its cloak around my shoulders as I looked across at the judge. I could have been an actor in my own play but without the dress rehearsal prior to the opening night. The same questions asked were ones I'd heard so many times before. The answers were always the same.

I was questioned again about Edmund's injury and what had happened that night just over a year ago in the bathroom at home. The other barristers asked about the failure to notice anything was wrong with him in the days leading up to his collapse and admission to hospital. They pointed out this was my third child and I should have been aware he was unwell. I had; he had been bringing back more feed than usual but not to the point of outright vomiting. He had appeared off colour for a few days and had been damp and clammy when I got him out of his cot in the mornings. I'd never been one of those nervous parents who took their children to the doctor at every sniffle.

The relationship with Mike, which had been painted as violent, was raised and why I'd stayed with him, even marrying him in spite of realising he had caused Ed's injury. I was allowed to answer, to process my thoughts with the deliberation which had been so often criticised in the past. It wasn't an indicator of seeking ways to fabricate deceit. In truth, it was my autism, unknown about at the time, which made answering much slower than could have been expected. Yet here, in the courtroom, it felt much easier somehow to explain motives, actions and everything else which occurred at the time.

Physically, the distance from the questioners was helpful as there was no feeling of personal space being invaded. Recalling the frequent interviews with the social workers, they'd often leaned forward, which made me feel nauseous and threatened. Remembering the interview in that dark little cave of a room in the hospital a year earlier and how intimidating it had been, the vast space of the courtroom seemed breathtaking. I'd crawled out of a sewer and was about to fly. The social workers, Ashley and Anne, even Paul, had given facts and asked about my feelings. Emotions were alien creatures I was frequently asked about but was confused on how to comment on. Here, in court, I was being asked for reasons behind my actions, not emotional responses.

It was strange to go home feeling elated. Rowena said it was going well and the judge liked me. How she could possibly tell was a mystery but naive hope caused me to grasp at any remotely positive straw. The positive straws, however, wouldn't have built a raft to carry an insect. The influence of Paul Hillingwood was heavyweight and the fact that the outcome of such cases usually swung in the favour of the Guardian ad Litem wasn't one to be ignored.

I rang the prayer chain for a third time, passing on news and knowing it would be passed on. I also rang Mr and Mrs Flint to enquire after Edmund. It was almost a week since I'd seen him. They said he was 'missing his mummy'. I was concerned he was getting insufficient fresh air. Brian and Kath were not ones to go out if it was too cold and the weather all week had been damp and drizzly, the way it always seemed to be at funerals. It was good to get away from the intense pall of the court where everyone's own little huddle stood back to back in a silent, suspicious feud.

The tone on Thursday changed. As much as we had gone home the previous day feeling the fresh air of an upwardly changing atmosphere, the fourth day was a gathering storm which swept in with the menace of a summer thunderstorm. David was in the witness box. As an older teenager and young man in his early 20s, he had served as a special constable for Nottinghamshire Police. I looked across the courtroom at David and saw a lifetime of memories in an instant.

Like our younger brother, David had been public school educated at a Quaker boarding school in West Yorkshire and his accent was testimony to having mixed in circles more affluent than ours had been. He had loved every day of his school life from the time he started. It allowed him space for personal development, provided structure, consistency and safety. It was also a haven from the bullying he received at home.

Dad, it seemed, had taken a dislike to his elder son, who was born with the umbilical cord strangling the life out of him. His face was turning black and Dad was convinced David was, in Mum's words, an imbecile and his behaviour towards our brother consistently swung between victimising him and overcompensating by buying gifts neither my sister nor I were privy to. Once we saw Dad taking David up the road, hand in hand. When they returned, David had a pedal car. David had the first bicycle too and was given individual attention as the eldest child in ways Jane and I never seemed to get. Somehow the family treated my sister and me like an inseparable unit. We were 'the girls'. Our brother, before Andrew was born, was simply David. Afterwards, they too were united in a singular and became 'the boys'.

Of course, the individual attention David gained created resentment in the family. Whilst I would have rarely strayed from the childhood bleating of 'not fair', Jane had other less pleasant ideas and adopted her own form of low-level bullying in the form of overt bossiness. The two siblings were never close. Being more inclined towards my brothers, we played together well when our sister was otherwise occupied, something which increased as we grew up. It was much nicer being one of 'the boys' than it was trying to be a girl, and the three of us, David, Andrew and me, would play outdoors together. One of our favourite games was exploring the wasteland at the back of the housing estate we lived on. We were usually either cowboys on horseback or space explorers. To us, the grey dusty hills created out of waste from the nearby coal mine looked like barren planets. I also used to visit the wasteland and play there on my own.

I felt both shame and pride as I looked across at David. He was smart, spoke with clarity and wasted no words in his answers. There was no room to doubt his resolute steadfastness in support of his family. From Edmund's admission to hospital, our stay at St Joseph's and visiting us at the Family Support Centre, his faithfulness and consistency never once waivered. The bond with his baby nephew was like iron, strong and unbending. At no time had he been duplicitous or acted for his own gain, other than to enjoy the time he spent with Ed. Never once had he expressed anger towards me for the part I, as a child, had played in his misery. I was ashamed of the way I'd behaved. Even in the hierarchy of childhood where the younger children copied the older ones, who emulated the attitudes of parents and grandparents, there was always room for rebellion but I never did.

David was asked if at any point he could have hurt Edmund, but the questioning was weak and he had never been seen as a likely perpetrator as his visits only began during the time in hospital. If anything, his total support was one of the very few unquestionable facts.

Then it was Mum's turn. She looked tiny in the witness box. Somebody asked her a question, "How would you describe the relationship between yourself and your daughter?" She paused slightly before answering, "A normal mother and daughter relationship." She was rounded on in an instant and it became horrifyingly obvious why I'd been coaxed to be 'open' and 'honest' so often. "So why has she been heard to say you beat her up throughout her childhood?" I'd been lured into weaving the rope which would hang me then tear my family apart.

It was true; Mum had been violent towards me and ultimately it was the reason I left home and Derek and I bought our first house together. That particular event came after years of never being quite good enough, of not being more like my sister or a real girl. "Why do you always have to have something wrong with you? Why can't you just be normal? Why do you always have to be different?" Worst of all was the insidious chipping away of self-esteem. There had been the lack of confidence displayed in me and her expectation of negativity.

She had never listened to my side of the story when I was accused of behaving badly. Trying to talk to her was one of the most painful things I ever had to do, growing up. I would stammer, cry and my words would get lost. Mum would laugh at me, mimic my stammer and say, "Spit it out." The hostility she showed me spilled over to her wider family, especially her own mother. It was no wonder I retreated into a world of imaginary friends, secret diaries and a hope that one day somebody would love me.

The beginning of the end of that particular chapter came when Mum announced one particular Monday morning that her boyfriend Jim and his son were moving in that Friday. What was most shocking was the lack of forewarning. I'd been the only one of four siblings living at home full time as my brothers were in boarding school and my sister had left more than a year earlier. As was common in the family, it seemed although I was the one most likely to be affected, I was also the last to know. Autistic people take to imposed changes quite badly and the family knew this, even though my autism was still unknown about. There was a blanket failure to provide forewarning over impending changes and their response to my general meltdown was, "We knew you'd be upset," as if that was ever a good reason to leave off telling me until the last possible moment. Growing up, I used to tearfully beg for more notice next time but it never came, so by the time I reached my mid-teens, my suffering was generally internalised.

My efforts to make the best of it went unnoticed. Clumsy as they probably were, I was trying. Mum's boyfriend seemed quite hostile but was probably heavily influenced by her negative opinion of me and there was quite a noticeable prejudice towards my relationship with Jim's son. They worked on the assumption I was angry with him and failed to see how much I was trying to make him feel at home. Robert was a very quiet boy and at 14 was very close in age to my younger brother. He was difficult to talk to and would only ever give one word answers to a question. He must have felt as awkward as the rest of us.

It all came to a head a few months later when my brothers were home for Christmas. Andrew, the younger one, had spent the day with a friend from our old neighbourhood and had been brought back home by the boy's grandmother. Derek, who I had been dating for a few months, had brought me home. The house was full of people. Robert was in the dining room playing music, the lounge was so full there was nowhere other than the windowsill to sit on, and Mum and Andrew's friend's grandmother sat at the kitchen table. I offered to make cups of tea for everyone and produced hot drinks for those who asked.

Shortly after returning to my windowsill seat, Mum stormed into the lounge demanding to know why I hadn't made a drink for Robert. With the television on in one room and music playing in another, I hadn't heard him ask. Apologising, I said I would make one but Mum snapped, "Too late, he's made it himself," and launched into an angry tirade of how I'd always 'had it in for Robert ever since he moved in' and how I was horrible to him.

Everything was the complete opposite of reality. I was shocked, hurt and angry. Suppressing the intense rage I felt, quietly and mostly under my breath I swore at her. She heard. Even before leaving the kitchen, I knew what was going to happen. Once she started thumping me, around my shoulders and the back of my head, I thought she would never stop. Her verbal abuse was similar to the kitchen rant but with an added, "You're just like your father, you are." I was silent under the attack and so was everyone else in the room. Nobody stopped her and nobody helped. When the thumping stopped, David, from his chair, said quietly, "If you have anything to say to her, why don't you take her somewhere else and have a quiet word?"

I was still crying the next day, not from the bruises but from the broken spirit and lack of justice. Derek, who had witnessed everything, said I didn't have to put up with that, we would find somewhere of our own to live. Mum had often told me I would never leave home because I'd nowhere to go but she was wrong. Somebody cared about me and wanted me to be safe.

Whatever thoughts Mum had from the witness box, she calmly answered question after question the barristers put to her. Her demeanour revealed nothing. Watching her, I wanted to shout out an apology for even thinking she had hated me, let alone tell anyone. She was there and that was one half of a bigger mystery. Why had she unquestioningly stood by me over the past months? At some point, I'd asked and she simply said she didn't want a grandchild of hers going to strangers. No support for me, she was doing it for herself.

She stood before the court and confirmed she would never suspect me of causing Edmund's injury. This was the first time there was even a suggestion she was making a vote of confidence in me either as a person or her daughter. What was 'a normal mother and daughter relationship'? I wondered what she meant by that and was it normal to seem to systematically seek out and destroy her child's self-esteem, as she seemed to have so badly wanted to do. This particular twist in the questioning left me cold and afraid.

Mum stood down from the witness box and the court broke for a quiet and gloomy lunch, after which Mum returned to the corridor and her knitting. I stood outside silently smoking a cigarette with David. Nothing could blow away the depressing turn of events from the morning and, heavy spirited, we went inside. David joined our mum and I returned to the courtroom. Anne and Ashley, sitting a few feet away further along the bench, radiated an exquisite kind of smugness which had begun in the morning. They sniggered and shared schoolgirl secrets with each other. An abused child is more likely to turn into an abuser. An opened chocolate wafer bar lay on the seat between them, which they surreptitiously ate when the judge's attention was on Yvonne.

If Mum's ordeal had been harrowing, it was a shadow of Yvonne's. Those seeking to have Edmund removed pounded her with relentless questions for the rest of the day and all of the next. Everything about her was astonishing. She was subjected to an intimate scrutiny of her professional credentials and probed over our relationship and had her judgment been clouded by it? She was questioned over the reasons behind her dismissal in the magistrates' court. Yvonne reiterated how she had been asked to conduct a forensic psychological assessment of Mike and me, which she had done. She hadn't suggested a likely perpetrator as this wasn't in the remit at that time. Instead, following on from her experiences of having her evidence discredited, she had continued working with me.

I had realised a relationship with Mike was untenable if I wanted Edmund to come home. Yvonne had supported me through the breakdown of my marriage and had treated me like a decent and intelligent human being. She had been someone I confidently placed trust in and she didn't let me down. Yvonne, with her smiling face, floral skirts, bright T-shirts, dangling earrings and openness had always been a source of light in the darkness. For a day and a half, I watched her in the witness box. Again, as had happened in the magistrates' court, her professionalism and integrity were in question. Heaven must have wept for her.

After five days in court, there was still more evidence to hear. The case was adjourned until the New Year. I'd spent a whole week listening to evidence; the first three days had looked promising but the last two threw everything into chaos and it was too much to think about. It was also Holly's sixth birthday and, for the second year in a row, her special day had been overshadowed.

As I'd done a few days earlier, I changed my clothes on the journey back. Changing into jeans while still wearing a skirt was difficult even without the added constraint of being in a moving car. Before we were out of town, I was dressed in my taxi driver clothes and ready for work. The bag of change was clicked into place at my waist. I had my job to go to. Mum dropped me at 'base', the taxi depot. I could have kissed the ground at every step it took to get from the car to my taxi and everything which had come to represent 'normal'.

Friday night was always busy. Life was a spider hanging from the thinnest of threads in the most inaccessible corner of the house. It wouldn't be swept away. I was glad of the banter in the supermarket car park where many of us gathered between jobs. After the week, it was grounding, refreshing and so incredibly welcome.

Monday was a mixture of gratitude at being back in a normal routine and excitement at seeing Edmund again. He was pleased to see me too. When I arrived at the Flints' house, he met me at the door. Kath did that: either she or Brian had my son in their arms when they welcomed me in so he was chest height and I could take him straight off them, which I did. We spoke a little about the proceedings the week before, but uncomfortably and in brief. In spite of their friendliness and hospitality, they nevertheless worked for the Social Services and could, for all I knew, somehow be human listening devices. There was never any knowing whether or not they would, innocently or otherwise, repeat something back to Ashley that would become twisted to reflect badly on me.

It was the same at the Family Support Centre. On the surface everyone was friendly but their job was to facilitate access between me and my son and him with his father and other members of the family. They were not supposed to show any bias and indeed didn't. There had been an occasion where I raised a concern about the bent paperclip Mike had used to repair a rip in his trousers, saying it could injure Edmund's bare legs. He had been in little shorts that day as it was hot. Nobody said anything and the next day his legs were bruised and scratched. None of these incidents had ever been written down.

The Family Support Centre had been decorated for Christmas during my week's absence. Although the impending festive season was interrupting the continuation of the court proceedings, it wasn't as difficult to live with as I might have expected. For one, it provided a break, as any more days in court would have been harrowing and it at least gave me a second Christmas with my son. Maybe it would be our last for as many years as it took for him to trace me in his adult years, so it was good to make the most of it and every day became a photo opportunity.

I took pictures of Edmund asleep in his buggy after the Support Centre play he was a star in. He was toddling around by then and had a fixation with anything vaguely mechanical, so got lots of fun from turning on the taps at the tiny bathroom washbasins, which I happily allowed him to do. Everything he did was a window in a microcosm and worthy of a photograph, even those in his high chair, when he fell asleep in his dinner, spoon still raised vertically in his chubby little hand. Most families have pictures like that but few expect them to ever be among the last they will take of their child. I was very aware these may have been such photographs.

January was both forever away and no time at all. I took Terran and Holly shopping so they could choose Christmas presents for Edmund. It was something fun to do because it involved visiting toy shops. They only saw their half-brother during school holidays so buying Christmas presents for him connected them all. Taking Terran and Holly out was a relief from the previous year when life had revolved around the room in the hospital. We were still based at the contact centre Derek had insisted on so getting around Nottingham city centre was easy to arrange.

It also became very busy at work with even Tuesday, a traditionally quiet evening for taxi drivers, getting quite hectic. Alongside regular customers, there was a lot of additional trade from people getting together with family and friends as midweek bookings in restaurants were usually cheaper than on Friday and Saturday nights. There were office party crowds to take home as employees chose to drink freely at the hair-down events and didn't want to drive. I was kept afloat by the jovial mood of most customers, who were positive and pleasant on the whole and therefore tipping a little more than average in a seasonal wave of goodwill. The seasonal decorations in towns and city centres gave brightness to the streets, especially when it rained and the roads and pavements reflected the colours of the Christmas lights.

There was also the drivers' night out to look forward to, which in company tradition was always on the Wednesday between Christmas and New Year and described by Tony the boss as 'the deadest night of the year'. In terms of work, it was very quiet as there was a natural lull from the chaos of Christmas before the New Year's Eve madness began. We were all being asked to cover shifts over the festive period. I was happy to sign up for everything. With nothing else to do and nowhere to go over Christmas and New Year, it helped other drivers who had families to celebrate with.

Perhaps that time should have been something to dread but I welcomed it. On a basic financial level, if Edmund came home it would mean extra money to save when I gave up my job, which was on my list of plans in the event of the unexpected happening. It also kept me busy. As any length of time spent dwelling on the awfulness of the situation filled me with fear, doing anything which drew my thoughts away from it helped to keep despair out and allowed space to breathe. The dancing, evening classes with Pascale, time out with my other children and, of course, work were all roads in to rebuilding a new life which Edmund would probably never become part of.

The older two of my children were kept informed over what was happening. They were given facts in as much of a straightforward way as possible, although exactly how much meaning it had for them was uncertain. Keeping the information simple and non-emotive worked well with them, as did being honest. They didn't seem at all worried or anxious when they were told Eddy had been hurt; they knew the authorities wanted to have him taken away and given to a new family but I was doing everything I could to stop it from happening.

They were invited to ask if there was anything they needed to know, and when they did, they were simple short replies. My children were among very few people I'd been able to be totally open with. They'd adapted really well to Edmund going from home to hospital, the mother and baby home and foster care. Where we met never seemed to be an issue for them as long as it happened.

Derek allowed me unsupervised access to the children on Christmas Eve and we went to see Edmund at the Flints' house. I booked a company taxi to fetch me and we collected Holly and Terran on the way. We were at Brian and Kath's for an hour or two and the two older children enjoyed playing with Edmund. I'd bought him a bright orange rocking aeroplane. He could just about manage to get on the seat without help. It had a blue steering wheel with a squeaky horn in the middle and there were levers on either wing that made ratchet noises when pushed backwards and forwards. The box it came in was enormous and, like all children, Ed loved it as much as the plane itself. He spent a long time crawling down to the bottom and back.

It was another photo opportunity and maybe the last time they were to be pictured together. They looked a total mash-up of characters with Terran in his army camouflage outfit and hat, Holly in the pink jumper she never seemed to take off. Edmund was still in his nightclothes. It was nice to have the older ones with me when we left as it helped to occupy the empty space that opened when we left the Flints.

For over a year, we had been living for the moment. Ever since Edmund had been taken into hospital, each point in his life became more precious, poignant. Everything bought for him could, in a few months, be wrapped and packed off into another life somewhere else, where some other couple would become 'mummy' and 'daddy'. Next year, another living room floor on an unexplored planet in another world would be littered with Edmund's bricks, stacking rings and lift-the-flap books. Was I consciously living the dreams from my childhood? Was buying those gifts giving him something to take into his next life? If I gave him enough, would there be something he would hold on to in a few years' time, knowing his old mummy in his other life, from another time and place, had given it to him?

We all walked back to the town centre, stopping at a café for something to eat before catching the bus home. We spent the rest of the day relaxing and playing together until it was time for me to go to work. One of the other drivers collected the three of us but he needed taking back to the taxi office before I could take the children and their gifts home. From outside their house I radioed through 'Car 17, clear Stapleford'. The radio operator came back with 'Thank you Car 17' and gave me my first job. Christmas had begun.

I pushed a tape into the car's cassette player and hit the road. It was a busy but fun night and with the fares being double, it was also very profitable. Most customers were in good spirits and even with the higher rates still gave me tips. To help passengers get into a festive mood, I put a bucket of sweets on the back seat. When it was quiet, I used the unofficial drivers' meeting place in the supermarket car park to catch up with the rest of the team.

Apart from the tips, customers would often share cigarettes with me, although it was generally so they were then allowed to smoke in the car as these were the days before workplace smoking was banned. It was also common to be offered slices of pizza, chips or a share in a takeaway meal. Sometimes I would find loose change from trouser pockets on the seats, which boosted my tips for that shift. I enjoyed the job enormously and was very happy with the firm I worked for and popular with the other drivers. Kevin and

Tony often used me as an example of how to work hard. Hard work meant more money for everyone, but the busier I kept myself, the less time I had to worry about my personal circumstances.

As Christmas fell on a Sunday that year, I'd worked the Friday as usual and had the benefit of double time after 6pm on Saturday. Shortly after 3am, I parked my car outside the house. I was home, tired but with a sense of fulfilment and peace. I made tea and toast, counted my money and walked my King Charles spaniel around the quiet streets before going to bed. The Christmas Day shift I was allocated began at midday so a decent sleep mattered. The shift was steadily busy and the money kept rolling in.

That evening I got together with a friend and we went out to Derby. We found an Indian restaurant open and had a curry. I'd known Iain for a number of years, as we used to live around the corner from each other. We had married in the same year, had our first children a few weeks apart, and separated from our respective partners at around the same time. He had been a very good friend since we met again by accident in a second-hand shop in the town shortly after Derek and I separated. He had been a very loyal friend to both Mike and me but was reluctant to get involved with the care proceedings as he knew Mike to be intimidating. After our meal, we went back to Iain's house and I spent the night on his sofa before going home early the next day.

The radio operator telephoned early on Boxing Day as work was starting to come in. Kevin and Tony were both in the office at the base when I took the taxi back that afternoon. They needed someone to take a young teenager back to a children's home in the north of the county and asked if I could do it. There would be time for a two-hour break and I rang Mum to ask if David, who was staying with her over Christmas, would make the trip with me, which he did. It was dark and the journey must have taken an hour each way on a very rural route, but was a very good job owing to the distance and the double fare.

Once back in radio contact, I was given another job then another and on it went until two o'clock in the morning. It was, even by my standards, an unusual Christmas but probably one of the best. New Year ran along a similarly busy pattern. Between 11pm and 12.30am the radio went quiet and the roads became still as revellers were at their destination, waiting for the countdown to midnight. Many of the drivers met up in the supermarket car park and we saw in the New Year together. In between those two weekends, however, had been the drivers' night out.

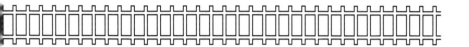

CHAPTER 14

Calling it drivers' night out made the event sound more inclusive than it actually was. Apart from me, there were no female drivers and wives and girlfriends were never invited. It was, in fact, another term for lads' night out. The other drivers and radio operators had been urging me to go, quite possibly as a joke. If it was, I missed the point and began to look forward to it. The Family Support Centre was closed for the Christmas holidays so seeing Edmund was limited to making short visits to the Flints' house and fitting in with their personal arrangements. There would be no need to get up early the next day.

Having no idea at all what to wear but keen to join the game, I came up with something I hoped would be just the right kind of outfit. I bought some leather shorts which went very nicely with the knee-high boots Mum had bought for me for Christmas. The regular walking, cycling, swimming and dancing had given me, at 33, the leanness of an athlete. A short blue front-tying blouse went over the top of a black satin all-in-one suit. The look was flattering and made the best of my legs without showing any bare flesh. It was a little cheeky but not overly flirtatious.

Having been working at what was essentially a man's job for a few months, I'd heard enough conversations between the other drivers to become acquainted with their attitudes towards and language describing young women's dress code and exposed body parts on weekend nights. Being the talk of the supermarket car park at quiet times was hardly anything to aspire to. Another thing to consider was the spectre of the Social Services ready to pass a negative judgment. However huge the relief of a respite away from the scrutiny I was constantly under, it was difficult to totally relax.

It was an added motivator to take care over my personal presentation, both in dress and behaviour, because if word got back to Ashley, anything negative that could have been made of it certainly would have been. The court hearing wasn't over and there was always the possibility either Kevin or Tony, as my bosses, could have been subpoenaed to appear in court. It had already been said that by taking on a job as a night-time taxi driver, I was putting myself at risk. There really were no entirely safe places to hide.

I was the first of the drivers to arrive at the pub we were meeting at. Ordering a Diet Coke at the bar, it was going to be a night on soft drinks. There was no way a little too much alcohol would lure me into anything a clear head would otherwise warn against. Being unsure how seriously to take the bawdy jokes, I'd laughingly said if I was going to get my backside squeezed, I needed to know whose face to slap. There had been women working for the taxi company before but, according to one of the radio operators, all of them had left with bad reputations. This was an imbalance in attitudes towards male and female behaviour. It was completely accepted that some of the drivers had 'lady friends', even the married ones, but frequently overhearing how they were talked about was somewhat unflattering.

THE JOURNEY OF AN AUTISTIC MOTHER

The pub started to fill up with off-duty taxi drivers; they arrived singly, two by two and in small groups. It was like the queue to get into Noah's Ark. The volume and atmosphere increased quickly as drinks were ordered and the banter began. One of the most enjoyable aspects of working in a male environment was the jokes and free exchange of overtly personal comments. In their clean shirts, pressed trousers, polished shoes, gelled hair and more fragrance than a department store, the guys were unrecognisable from the bunch of blokes I worked with. It was hard to imagine them sitting around the town in their cars, smoking one cigarette after another, waiting for their taxi number to be called.

Seeing smart versions of men who were more usually seen around town in dirty jackets and scruffy pullovers was much more of a contrast than would be found in an average office party; presumably as much of a novelty was how I was dressed, in fishnet hold-up stockings, leather boots, spiked hair and body glitter. It elicited a pleasantly surprised response of, "Oooh, she's got legs." On many levels, they were wonderful to see, as each one came not only as part of a team worth working for, each one made the darkest time of my life bearable.

Beside the drivers, Kevin had invited two other friends along, both male. One of them was very tall, well over six feet, quite thin but nevertheless good looking. The other of Kev's friends, a slightly paunchy, dark-haired man, warned me his friend was 'a bit of a Romeo'. He was right. This one, Gary, moved in quickly and manoeuvred every situation and scenario which followed to stay as close as he possibly could.

A fleet of taxis took us all to a pub in Nottingham, where Kevin bought drinks for everyone. I spent a little time talking to Mark, the youngest radio operator. He was about ten years younger than me but was more accustomed to living the night life than I was and was drinking something I never knew existed. From there, another fleet

125

took us to a different pub, where there was a strip show on. It was something, apparently, Tony insisted on. I became uncomfortable.

I stood outside while the act was taking off her clothes and rubbing herself in baby oil to the whistles and cat calls of 'the lads'. Being late December, it was very cold but I stood outside, lit a cigarette and shivered. Gary, in an effort to win favours, kept me company and continued to be at my side all night. We were only there long enough for Tony and the other drivers to whistle and leer at the act and down a few more drinks. More taxis arrived and we all piled into and out again just minutes later at a city nightclub. This was all new, exciting, amazing.

Nottingham was full of Christmas lights and everything seemed bright and mysterious in the cold and dark. The difference switching from driver to driven was rather like changing from mouse to cat. It was my turn to chase some fun. I spent much of the evening on the dance floor, most of it with Gary, who was quite difficult to escape from but it was only diplomatic to dance with my work colleagues. Their attempts to pull me closer were comic. One or two tried to grab my bottom but I was very quick on my feet and agile as a hungry leopard. It was good to be free and stay that way.

Like many experiences during that time, it was a rest from the stresses of being under surveillance. I was a person, a human being, one who was trying to stay alive and sane and who wished, more than anything, to win for her son the chance to know his family. Every happy moment, as there had been many since Eddy was placed back in foster care, was edged with fear and uncertainty. The duplicity of involved parties had made me paranoid and mistrustful. On the surface, so many of them had spoken positive, encouraging words; mantras such as being open and honest meant very little. They were obscure statements which time proved to be lies and deception. I trusted too quickly; I'd been naive.

The social workers seemed to judge me badly for doing anything which spoke of life and love, freedom and joy. Any laughter or pleasure was seen as coming from someone taking the seriousness of the court and care proceedings far too lightly. It was like being all of the three little pigs at once; I'd gone from the house of straw to the stick house and now it was made of brick. The wolf was howling at the door, trying to get in and snatch Edmund away.

There was also Sean to consider. He was a police officer I'd met some months earlier, when Mike had broken into the garden shed during the night and stolen my bicycle. I'd become quite a familiar visitor at the local police station as Mike had, at one point, got into the habit of stalking me, as he had when he appeared in the church hall those months earlier. The front desk staff became so used to my regular appearances one of them said, on seeing me, "25 Waterloo Street, isn't it? What's he done now?"

The bike was returned but after that Sean kept turning up. I would see him at night sometimes, when I was out at work. The police station was opposite the supermarket car park where the drivers often gathered and we often watched, from our idling taxis, police cars and foot officers going to and from the station. He advised carrying a deodorant spray of some kind in the top pocket of my jacket. Whilst it was against the law to carry an obvious weapon to fight off a potential attacker, it was acceptable to use something in self-defence that was reasonable to expect anyone to carry.

I couldn't get in my house one day. Something had come apart in the door mechanism and, although unlocked, it wouldn't open. Pushing and pulling at the handle had no effect. My little King Charles spaniel stood patiently at my feet while I fiddled with the back door lock. He went almost everywhere with me and was friendly and welcoming at the end of the day, after contact visits with Edmund. He would get walked in the small hours of the morning as a break between finishing work and going to bed. He was treated to extra long outings on Sunday afternoons and days off.

Not knowing what else to do, I walked with my dog to the police station and asked for Sean. He had given me his shift times a few days earlier when I went to report the bicycle theft. He brought me home in a police car. I sat in the back, holding the dog on my lap. My house was only half a mile from the police station so the journey was short and almost silent.

After rattling the handle and turning the key a few times, Sean agreed it was unlocked but the door mechanism had collapsed. He said there was only one thing for it. Lifting one leg to hip height, he gave the door a quick kick. Almost as though an invisible person was answering the knock, it opened. Sean stood upright, smiled and asked if I had a screwdriver. While he took apart the lock, we laughed about it and chatted. He found the whole thing quite exciting.

Besides talking about the difficulty with the door, we talked about his life and interests. He was born to an English mother and New Zealander father. His parents had met on a boat travelling to England. Sean, although born in the UK, was raised in New Zealand from early childhood. About two years younger than me, we had a lot in common, like cycling, walking and tastes in music. He also liked running and had twice taken part in Iron Man triathlons in New Zealand.

Shortly after that, he was beaten up while on duty and sustained facial injuries. The incident was reported in the local press. I sent him a card.

It's often difficult to remember how and why friendships develop but he, apparently, was recovering from the breakdown of a long-term relationship. I was in need of friends and we enjoyed one another's company. Maybe I was in need of someone to look after me, but it was easy to let it slip to everyone at the Family Support Centre that I'd made friends with a local police officer. It was almost like playing to the audience as I was sure of the possibility something would be written down, somewhere, that I'd become friends with such an upstanding member of the community. To have such a friend surely would have demonstrated my ability to form acceptable friendships and make positive life choices.

Nothing about any of this was reported on, anywhere. Allowing Mike to think Sean was a new boyfriend very effectively deterred any further harassment from him. He had been on the wrong side of the law too many times to see the police as anything other than the enemy. It was light, easy and refreshing to be away, for just a few hours, from the stress of the issues surrounding Edmund. Our relationship became rewarding and reciprocal in its nature. It was also platonic, at least to begin with.

Sean invited me over to his house for dinner, which was something to look forward to. He drove over to collect me. The total novelty of being treated with such respect was quite flattering. There had been few opportunities to visit anyone's house socially for some time and it was nice to relax, to have an evening off. I'd been invited, occasionally, to Maureen's house for Sunday dinner but that felt more like an act of kindness rather than friendship. This was different. This was somebody my own age.

Sean put on a CD to play, one of my all-time favourite albums, *Automatic for the People* by REM, and left me in the lounge while he went to put the finishing touches to the dinner. Everything in Sean's house was modern, very neat, tidy and meticulously arranged. There were dark tartan checked sofas in a contemporary design placed opposite each other with a coffee table in between, with a handful of lifestyle magazines on it. It looked like a room scene from an Ikea catalogue. Through the window, which stretched across one side of the room, was a small garden. Beyond that, a row of mature poplar trees in full leaf swayed in the breeze. Sean said he often like to lie on the sofa, looking through the window, watching them.

Nobody was spying; nobody was writing anything down to go into a twisted report. Had they done so, they would have only noted two people in their early 30s enjoying an evening together. We ate in the small dining kitchen, overlooked by Boris, Sean's pet tarantula, which lived in a small glass tank on top of the fridge. The meal, consistent with everything else about Sean and his house, was neat and tidy. The carrots were cut into small sticks and carefully arranged alongside the broccoli on the plate.

The conversation between us was lively and stimulating. Sean had spent four years at university in New Zealand gaining a degree in psychology, and alongside our similar interests in music and cycling this gave us a lot to talk about. At the end of the evening, he drove me back home. I felt as though I'd been away for weeks on a long, happy holiday in the sun somewhere. He was preparing to go back to New Zealand for a holiday, to stay with his father and see family and friends, and in the weeks leading up to this we saw quite a lot of each other.

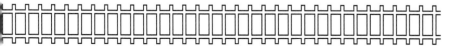

CHAPTER 15

The court hearing resumed. Leicester County Court was directly opposite the railway station and close to several multi-storey car parks. The court building itself was behind one of those car parks and a much larger, far more modern court than the first one had been. It was still dark and cold but, many years later, I wondered if the gloom and chill were more psychological. There would be only a few more days before everything that would be said had been said and all evidence presented.

We stood around a seating area in the corridor. David couldn't spare any more days away from his studies and had returned to college. Mum had to return to work. Fay couldn't be there either but Margaret, her secretary, was. She had been the one to give me a lift to court and would do so for the three days we were expecting the remainder of the hearing to last.

Leicester seemed a long way from home and very alien. It was where my appointments with Anna had been. Rowena, naturally, was also present and so was another familiar face, one I hadn't been expecting: Dr Holden, the psychiatrist I'd visited for my eating disorders and someone I hadn't seen for 18 months. He had discharged me before I fell pregnant with Edmund because keeping appointments became difficult once my job as a residential social worker got underway. Besides which, the bulimia he had been treating me for ended at around the same time as my marriage to Derek. Why was he there?

He was a slimly built man of about my own height so it was easy to look him in the face. With no smile or word of greeting, I said, "Whose side are you on?" I looked over my shoulder at the social workers in their muttering huddle with their legal team. Neil Holden said he had been subpoenaed by the Social Services to give evidence. We were called into court and I left my former doctor out in the cold waiting area. When he was called, I hoped very much there was nothing about our meetings which had led him to believe I was dangerous to children or, in fact, anyone else. Even though I had no history of violence, there had been far too many times since Edmund went to hospital where much had been made out of the smallest morsel of understandable upsets.

Dr Holden wasn't kept in the witness box for very long and there was no chance afterwards to speak to him either politely or otherwise. He said nothing to those questioning him he hadn't said to me during our meetings apart from one thing: I was, in his opinion, more likely to hurt myself than anyone else. He was questioned in depth about eating disorders and how bulimia nervosa had manifested itself in me. The doctor found it very unlikely that I would harm my own baby. The nature of an eating disorder was essentially, in my case, a form of self-harm. He had nothing to say regarding Mike as they'd never met.

The three days in Leicester passed quickly. The witnesses called after Dr Holden had nothing new to add. Some were positive and others less so, which gave neither side any apparent edge over the other. They were 'add-on' days where the last of the evidence was heard and witnesses came and went. Because my days were spent in the courtroom, with only recesses to break the time, witnesses entered, gave their oath and left without me ever having seen them in the waiting area. It was as though everyone had grown tired of the train of people chugging into the witness box station, answering their questions and gasping with relief on their way out. The points were set and no sudden change of direction emerged.

There was also an atmosphere of tiredness and irritation that this had stretched on for so long. Edmund was approaching 16 months old and a toddler. He had teeth, could speak a few words and was looking less like a baby. It was taking up time and resources and it seemed as though Ashley wanted to get the inevitable over with to allow Edmund his new life, with a new family. She made me feel guilty for refusing to admit the fight was useless.

The court almost always decided in favour of the Guardian ad Litem, who was clearly pushing for adoption, and my stubbornness was the stumbling block to that. Had it not been for my difficult behaviour, which is what seemed to be implied, Edmund would have been with a new family a year earlier and I was causing unhappiness to a couple longing for a child of their own.

Having been brought up hearing from my mother and others how selfish I was with barely a kind word from anyone created a lot of confusion and inner conflict. Where did selfishness begin and end and was it just a matter of perspective? Maybe the most unselfish act would have been to meekly and tearfully hand over my son knowing, even though I hadn't caused his injury, it was never going to be possible to raise a child on my own. To counter that thought, would it have been seen as selfish to deny Terran, Holly and Edmund the chance to know each other and share the things siblings do? Was it selfish to seek out and find a happy family life and if so, who was selfish and who wasn't? The family who wanted my baby or me for trying to keep him?

Most of this angst was internalised as trying to talk it through added to the pain. Everyone had their own agendas and motives and almost all absolved themselves by stepping back into comments such as 'only you can make that decision' and 'it's not up to me to tell you what to do'. Confused thoughts and emotions were never far away. They woke with me and nagged me to sleep. It was almost as though they'd been arguing through the night. Yvonne was the only person to truly trust. The only time my thoughts balanced was during our sessions.

The day the judge's decision came out was like being in labour all over again. Pacing the dining room of my house where 15 months earlier my son had been born was as painful as it had been then, but this was another kind of agony. Even the sofa he came into the world on was in the same place, along the wall which had doors at either end; one led upstairs and the other to the front of the house. A music system had replaced the television which Mike had taken when he left. Not that I would have watched it anyway. The radio was on but it was tinnitus as I enacted every possible response to the impending outcome.

As I paced, every conceivable scenario was rehearsed to the win or lose result. There was never going to be anything other than good news or bad. I drank coffee and paced, barely daring to leave the room in case I missed hearing the telephone ring. The carpet was the same, the walls were the same but it was daylight and I was on my own. There was no Mike, no midwives, no *Hotel California,* no gas and air to take away the pain. Maybe there would be no baby to hold and kiss at the end of it either. I paced and prayed a futile prayer, knowing however close my mouth was to God's divine ear, the decision was made. Maybe it was all very reminiscent of being the last to know and the most involved, as had happened so often growing up.

It was Wednesday 25th January which wasn't a day I would have spent with Edmund. Morning went and afternoon came. The wait for Margaret, Fay's secretary, to ring as soon as the fax came through from the judge continued. Did Anne and Ashley feel as sick with apprehension as I did? Remembering them sitting in court, sneaking pieces of chocolate to each other and how they nudged and whispered during the eight days of the hearing, it was doubtful. They were probably looking forward to it, to having a nice white British baby to find a new home for. Their job satisfaction, however unjustly gained, must have been riding high on the proud stallion of self-righteous assumption.

I wondered where Mike was and how he was feeling. How were my mother and brother? Yvonne and my friends in the church and on the prayer chain were also waiting for the news. I was marching around under a rock. Heavy with every kind of pain, I willed and wished and dreaded the phone call. Edmund was no doubt happy doing the usual kind of things he did on days when he wasn't at the Family Support Centre. I thought about him, oblivious to the wait, the news that would change the course of his life, everyone's life.

Halfway through the afternoon, I called Maureen. Unable to carry the tremendous weight alone anymore, I asked if she was home and asked if I could go round. I rang Margaret, giving her the alternative number to call. There was still no news. Maureen, in her usual quiet calmness, carried on with her household tasks while I paced again, this time around the dining area of her kitchen. The company was a relief and that she neither indulged nor ignored me was comforting. There were no words to say as nothing could have helped. It was like standing for hours, blindfolded, in front of a firing squad, waiting for a rain of bullets to rip in and end my life.

The telephone rang. Time stopped. I stopped pacing. Maureen answered it. She was a hundred miles away, or so it seemed. I could hear her voice as though she was speaking through the wide end of a megaphone. "Yes she is, she's here," and gave the phone to me. It was the longest walk I'd ever taken. The time for execution had come and I gripped the telephone receiver in anticipation of the gunshot. It was Margaret, calling from the solicitors' offices. Somewhere else, Anne, Ashley and Paul were probably receiving similar calls. Mike's solicitor was no doubt also receiving the news. She said the report was appearing on the fax machine and she had the document with her. Carefully, I listened as Margaret read through the last of the 22-page finding. Was it going to make any sense?

If Edmund were subject to a care order and was placed for adoption, he would, under present plans, be removed from his mother and the extended family... such a step should only be taken if it is manifestly necessary in order to protect him... In my judgment it is far from established that the risks present here in returning him to her are of the degree which would justify such a drastic step as to require that he be adopted. I am satisfied that a Supervision Order is the appropriate order, with steps being taken to return Edmund to his mother's care in a structured way.

Barely able to breathe, sick with shock and holding my hand over the telephone receiver, I whispered to my friend, "We won." The tension broke in Maureen's dining kitchen. Her eldest daughter came in through the front door at that moment, interrupting the stunned joy. She squealed with delight when her mother broke the news. The atmosphere was congratulatory but quiet. We were all too numbed to do anything else. A ticker tape Hollywood moment this wasn't; there were no fireworks, no firing of cannon or cheers from an invisible crowd. For months, I'd played out one scenario after another in expectation of this day but not one of them had been anything like the reality.

Assuring Maureen I would be fine, I set out for the half-mile walk to the solicitors' offices, which took me towards the town centre and past the Social Services building where Ashley and Anne were, I imagined, sitting either side of a cauldron like twin witches, brewing their next move.

Judge David Browning had been very thorough. Rowena had anticipated this as he had to be seen to have examined all witness evidence and carefully considered everything before him. She had been correct in assuming he would wish to make a finding on the perpetrator of Edmund's injury. He had: Mike, which is what most had recognised almost 18 months earlier, when everything had begun. He couldn't be charged with the offence as there was no direct evidence, such as an admission or marks on Edmund's body, to link him to it. Had there been, the issue would have been concluded over a year earlier and little of what happened as a consequence would have occurred.

About me, he said, '.... *throughout the length of the hearing she remained calm and listened to the evidence without any display of temper or indeed emotion which so often characterises parents in these highly-charged cases where the decision can be of such profound significance for their future life. She conducted herself with impressive dignity*'. Regarding Yvonne, he had found her, in contrast to the dismissal at the magistrates' court, to be a credible witness. Thinking back to the ordeal she had undergone in court, this was exceptionally good news.

Fay saw me briefly, smiling and offering cautious congratulations along with a warning. I couldn't simply go and fetch Edmund as he had to be reintroduced to my home environment slowly and there were still procedures to follow. We still had to be seen to be cooperating with the authorities. It also gave me, from a far stronger position, a chance to prove my worth and credibility. On a practical level, there were preparations to be made at home and it was too much to expect a small child to be able to adjust immediately to being in a strange place. He had been moved around enough in his 16 months of life.

The other parties had 28 days to appeal. Given the thoroughness and approaches the judge had taken, my solicitor saw few grounds for argument, but argue they did. Fay rang with the unwelcome news. Twenty days after the judge's decision came through an appeal was lodged.

For almost three weeks, the routines had carried on as normal: visiting Edmund on every weekday apart from Wednesday, work on Tuesday, Friday and Saturday night and the consistent involvement from my brother and mother. In spite of this, the world seemed somehow less hostile and much friendlier; everything was warmer, brighter and had the fresh promise of impending spring. Now there was to be an appeal. Fay tried to explain the reasons but these made no sense. They were based on perceived errors by the judge and Yvonne's report and relationship with me. It also upheld the authenticity of the Guardian ad Litem and Anna Morris.

Before the Court of Appeal date, there was a hearing, back in Leicester, where those lodging it laid out their reasons. Mum didn't go and neither did David. There would have been no point as only those concerned would have been allowed to sit in on the hearing, just as it had been previously. Maureen gave me a lift. On the way down the motorway, I slid into a monologue as she drove, one which had been recited many times. Even though nobody had been charged for causing the assault on Edmund, we had indeed been on trial. Our, especially my, judgment was questioned time and again, we had been subjected to a great deal of scrutiny and every discovered response to stress, either in an angry outburst or tears, had been written down and reported on, yet no fault with my parenting had been found. The despair of being unable to prove I hadn't caused the original injury had been ongoing and painful. Did anyone have any idea how dreadful it felt to be guilty until they could prove they were innocent?

The hearing came and went in a litany of almost defamatory comments. The Social Services claimed not to accept the judge's findings at all and, furthermore, even should I have been an innocent party, they stated it highly possible I would enter into further violent relationships, as though the one with Mike had been only one in a trail of tragedy and torment. Additionally, they considered my mental health reason enough to render me unfit to raise a child on my own. If my autism been known about at that time, there is no doubt that this too would have been used against me.

It was as though they were determined to take away my baby using whatever available means were open to them and this felt very much like intimidation. At the same time, their bleating sounded hollow, like a wave from a severed arm. Ashley had often told me I stood no chance but the judge decided in my favour. Was this their last twist of the knife? Had these people no idea this was a fight for life? Were they actually concerned about this one child's welfare and future or were they simply trying to win him to tick a box on a form somewhere, or use the case as proof of their effectiveness?

It was for my children, all of them, not just Edmund that I needed to win. In all of the scenarios I rehearsed, mentally recorded and played back many times over the past months, an appeal had never featured at all. The winning and losing scenarios and all possibilities and endings were tried out, tested and judged for their emotional content. There had always been unrehearsed, unscripted dialogue and at each turn, more waiting, more decisions and more people to involve. Originally, I'd expected the court hearing, at its close, to recess while the judge retired to reach his decision. This hadn't been the case and when it came there was still the wait for the decision to appeal, which had been delayed by Paul, the Guardian ad Litem, being away on holiday.

Had I been told that an appeal was a possibility? Maybe, or perhaps it had been taken for granted I knew about it. Possibly Fay had intuitively known that too much information at one time would have overloaded me and had kept me informed of alternative possibilities on a need-to-know basis. This still meant that nothing was certain and there was still a long wait ahead.

The rock I'd marched under while waiting for the judge's decision was now the one I was dashed against. An appeal was one thing but the court was in London. I hadn't been aware of that because it had never been relevant. Words I'd only heard on the news were becoming real. Non-accidental meant *deliberate*; an *appeal* meant going to London. There was only one Court of Appeal. Ever since Edmund was admitted to hospital I was thrown into a culture which meant nothing to me, which had a language of its own. I was naive and vulnerable, afraid; what did these people want from me? All I wanted to do was show them how much I loved my baby, how I could care for him. I wanted to take him home. How was I going to get to London? It was a big place.

I walked from home to the town centre with tears like volcanic lava hitting my cheeks. The weeks since the end of the court hearing had been the most turbulent and emotionally draining since the time around Edmund's weeks in hospital and the period which saw us through the two weeks in the first foster home to our stay in St Joseph's. The ten months he had been with the Flints had been stable and a comfortable, although not always easy, routine had been established.

There was another telephone call from the solicitors' office and one which I'd never imagined happening. I had to go and see Fay as soon as possible. It sounded urgent, which was always concerning. The appeal had been dropped. It was suddenly hard to focus my thoughts. It was as though the walls, floor and ceiling were moving in and out, up and down while the light was repeatedly switched off and then on again.

It was the miracle I'd hoped for but could never imagine happening. The train, which had been idling in the sidings, began to move again and gathered speed. Edmund was coming home. Nothing happened quickly.

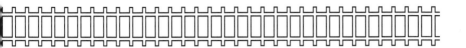

CHAPTER 16

Life was changing. Faced with the prospect of becoming a single parent of a toddler, it was a relief to have time to plan Edmund's homecoming. Nothing happened without a meeting and plans being put in place. There would be a gradual introduction back into the home environment because Ed had no memory of the house or area. It was one thing to remove him quickly and another to put him back. He would be brought to the house with the Flints and accompanied by Ashley, who remained artificially friendly and smiling. It was nice to be able to smile back from a new position, one of strength rather than vulnerability.

After a while, Edmund would be brought to the house without Brian and Kath so it would be possible for my son to become familiar with me on his own. We would be given a new social worker. Although this was supposed to provide a new start, a 'clean sheet', it was superficial. If it was ever going to be the best outcome it was nevertheless shallow, at least in my eyes.

I'd won my baby but lost my husband. Edmund was also to remain on the child protection register because he was returned home on a supervision order. This was explained to me but made no sense. He was coming home and there was nothing to worry about. As

I hadn't caused his injury and was more than able to take care of him, it was, in my mind, purely academic and something to demonstrate that, by continuing to offer full cooperation, there was nothing to be concerned about regarding his wellbeing.

We would still have to attend the Family Support Centre but fewer days a week, just two instead of the four we had been used to. It was suggested we transfer to the centre near home, as it was local and walking distance from the house. I declined. As had been the case with my children and throughout the part of my life I'd had control of, I'd always changed as little as possible at any one time. It would be enough for Edmund to make the move home so continuing to go over to the centre he was familiar with would cause less disruption.

Finally seeing Edmund at home brought mixed emotions. There would be a different kind of family life from the one I had imagined after Eddy's birth. Mike would clearly not be there. Our son would, however, grow up knowing his brother, sister and wider family. Nothing could take that away. It would again become possible for Terran and Holly to visit the house without my mum having to bring them to spend the day with us. They would be able to stay overnight, something they hadn't been able to do for almost a year and a half.

The slow transition home came to a rapid end when Edmund began to show distress. His routine had changed and it appeared to be disturbing him. When he was home he was happy but began to lose his sleep routine back at the Flints and became clingy. He had lived with them for almost a year and was very attached to them. It had been pointed out that to disrupt attachments in children was particularly traumatic for them to deal with at around six months and 18 months of age, key stages in their development. Edmund had been five months old when he went to live with Brian and

Kath and 17 months old when being introduced back home. It was hardly surprising he was getting upset. Of course, his own autism hadn't become apparent at that time, which would have added another layer of reason to his disturbance at the changes he was undergoing. There was nothing else for it but to bring him home early and cut short the transition period. Suddenly the slow-burning fire flickered into life.

The Flints sent Edmund back with his clothes in black dustbin liners. Most of the toys bought for him during his 11 months there came too. Brian and Kath also gave him the pushchair he had been using while living with them. They were upset to see him go but we promised to keep in touch, thinking it was better for Edmund to have contact with them at least occasionally. They'd been mummy Kath and daddy Brian for most of his life and, even though their lifestyle and parenting was a very different style from mine, they'd looked after him, loved and cared for him, and equally importantly, allowed not just Mike and me into their home and lives but Terran, Holly, my mum and brother too.

The whole family were upset to see Edmund go but it was the best of all the outcomes, or so we thought. The Social Services seemed to disagree. On her first visit, Janice, the new social worker, sat next to me on the sofa in the dining room, the one Edmund had been born on, and told me they still didn't know who had caused Edmund's head injury. I was stunned. I wanted to ask her to leave. After everything, the Social Services would still not acknowledge the findings set out by Judge Browning. It was no longer my business to convince anyone of my parenting ability or competency as a human being but theirs to prove I wasn't. Edmund was home. That was enough.

Mike never took up any contact although it was offered. He did, however, take to occasionally following us around the town centre.

A few days after his return home, it was Mother's Day. My boy was 18 months old. Derek brought Terran and Holly over so the three of us could enjoy the day. There could have been no better way than to celebrate together. Perhaps it should have felt strange to be at home with them and unsupervised for the first time in a year and a half but it didn't. It felt the way it should, real and natural, fun and nothing forced. If one of them overstepped a boundary, they were told off. The children seemed not to have any sense of ceremony because, like children do, they took it all in and enjoyed the day. Mum came over and had bought gifts to give from Edmund. Another friend, Maria, who I knew from the church group, brought something round. It was a circular pink soapstone box with a slightly ill-fitting lid. These were precious things to mark a special occasion which passed with neither sentiment nor tears.

Routines, as they'd been for my grandparents, were things which had always held a lot of importance, as was understanding the significance of changing as little as possible at any one time. Edmund knew me but the house was strange to him, which was the reason I opted to keep him at the same Family Support Centre. We slowly became used to a new way of life.

Edmund liked exploring his new environment on his own and disappear off, hunting around and discovering new things, which he seemed to really enjoy. Every now and again he could be heard calling "Mummy" from somewhere in the house. I called back "Edmund" and left him to carry on. Occasionally, I would shout back, "Right! I'm coming to find you." He thought it was hilarious. I took my camera with me one time and found him, grinning, standing in the built-in wardrobe in my bedroom.

His days with me were happy but there were a few dark shadows in his life. He was reluctant to be left alone at bedtime and would stand in his cot, banging its sides and crying endlessly. This required a new routine. After bath time, we would sit on the side of one of the beds in his room. Besides his cot, there were two beds that Terran and Holly used when they stayed over. We would cuddle while drying and dressing him in his nightclothes, then I read a few stories. Holding him tightly in my arms, we rocked together and I sang him to sleep, my lips pressed against his head. Moments such as those infused my soul with peace. Love for my boy rolled like the gentle kiss of a warm and fragrant breeze. When he was asleep, I laid him in his cot and waited a while, watching him.

We continued the same routine for a few days, then instead of singing him to sleep in my arms, I put him to bed and sang, leaving the room after his eyes had closed and he was quiet. From there we progressed through the bath time and story ritual to being put into bed before the singing. Eventually, it became possible to put Eddy to bed awake and leave him. Introducing him to a new environment and system of parenting in such a gentle way was far kinder than leaving him to cry. He had been traumatised enough.

It was a similar thing at the Family Support Centre. While Edmund had been living with the Flints he had accepted me leaving him but something changed when he came home. I could no longer even stand up without him clinging to my legs, bouncing up and down to be picked up and crying for all his worth. He was inconsolable. Against the advice of the Support Centre staff, he came with me. "He'll cry for as long as he has to, then he'll settle back down," I said. As tiresome as it was to have to take Edmund with me when I left the room, it seemed harsh to add to his suffering. It was actually quite empowering to be able to make a decision and follow it through. Eventually, and as a response to Edmund's distress in the Family Support Centre, he was moved to the one close to home. The clingy behaviour and tearful reactions stopped immediately. We really were on our way to a new life.

I tried introducing Ed to a parent and toddler group which met at the church. It was loud and very noisy; it was also nothing we needed. Large group situations have always been difficult for me, as they are with anyone on the autistic spectrum. Gauging and measuring how to respond, who to approach and whether or not to stand or sit are things which most people know how to do automatically, but social interactions are not second nature to everyone. We only went once. Nobody spoke to us and it was impossible to move without the clingy reaction from Edmund. He had been institutionalised enough. What he really needed was to be in other people's houses so we joined a group that met around members' homes.

Parents would meet to enjoy social chat, refreshments and maybe a craft activity while the children played. Edmund, as he was at home, was content to wander around on his own and showed no interest in social activities, the other children or even me but was hypnotised by the household gadgets. He had had so little experience of being in other people's houses he became almost clockwork, mechanical and went from the living room to the kitchen, pressing buttons, turning switches, fascinated by the moving parts of television sets, video recorders, the washing machine, cooker and almost anything else with a light, button or dial on it. He ignored the other children, their games and the toys. The sight of familiar objects in new places overawed him. His focus was so intense that nothing else mattered.

It was a time of rest. Those first few months at home saw the start and finish of spring and the onset of summer. Along with it came warmer weather and time for long walks. Mum visited every week and David often came over at weekends. We would take Edmund out in the buggy Mr and Mrs Flint gave us. The pushchair he had used throughout our stay at St Joseph's was one I'd picked up from a second-hand shop in Bath. Mike and I had gone over there one weekend to visit his mother. It was an amazing design as the seat could be clipped on to be either front or rear facing. Its fault was the wheels were quite weak and one had broken, and it only folded in half which meant collapsing it to use on the bus was tricky. Brian and Kath gave me the one they'd used for him during his stay there and it had been very welcome. I liked the transference of familiar objects from one place to another, it gave continuity. They also gave me the sit-in plastic car he had loved so much.

Taking Edmund out without having to be either supervised or back within a short timeframe remained a novelty for a very long time, so when we went out we stayed out and walked all afternoon. The dog came too, and we all got a great deal out of the fresh air. It certainly helped Edmund to sleep.

David and I came home from one of those long walks with a very tired Edmund who, as he sat at the table eating his supper, slowly began to fall asleep. We watched him, his face red from fatigue, as his eyes closed and he began to slip not just into a deep sleep but from his chair. Given his age and size, I'd decided getting a high chair was a waste of money and simply used a booster seat on a dining chair. It was from this that Ed was falling. Very quietly and carefully, David gently took hold of his nephew and caught him just before the boy went horizontal. He never woke once as David lifted him and took him over to the sofa. It was one of many peaceful and beautiful moments which formed, as Mother's Day had, a pleasant backdrop to the middle part of that year.

Shortly before Edmund's return home and prior to leaving my taxi driving job, a customer gave me an impressive tip, large enough to buy a child seat to go on the back of my bike. Buying his first little helmet brought back happy memories from when Terran and Holly were younger and travelled in the seat behind me. We were going to be mobile. Edmund would get the fresh air I was desperate for him to enjoy while he was away and had spent far too much time indoors.

With Eddy secure in the child seat, we rode around the area, discovering parks along the cycle route which ran alongside the river Derwent and into Derby. On days when Ed was fractious, cycling was a great soother for both of us. He was settled and happy at home but he had been through a big upheaval which sometimes seemed to catch up with him, disturbing both his behaviour and sleep. Cycling also proved to be good therapy for me as I would be occasionally gripped with angry thoughts about the situation we had been freed from. On days like those I would put Eddy in the bike seat and ride for 10, 15 or 20 miles until the anger went away.

I was also still seeing Yvonne, who would sometimes come to my house for lunch. At other times I would cycle to Nottingham and across the city centre to her clinic, taking Edmund with me. She witnessed the growing bond between us and how I was adapting to his changing needs and the new home life we were building away from the negative scrutiny of the authorities. She came on a reunion dinner we had for those whose support had been so important. Maureen was there and so was Fay, my solicitor.

It was always Yvonne, though, who held the biggest place in my heart. Fay, although having been a friend for so many years, had been acting as per her job role. She was risking nothing. Yvonne, however, had risked her professional reputation by refusing to be bought by the Social Services. Meeting her again many years later, I thanked her for her help. In my mind she had given me the right to a family life and for Edmund to know his birth family. The gratitude I have for this warm, honest and decent human being has remained. The trust put in her never wavered and she never let me down.

Throughout his stay in the foster home, Ed had had a sore chin from constant dribbling and I thought at first it was teething, but the rash cleared up during his first weeks at home and so did his spotty complexion. The mix of being away from people who smoked, getting more fresh air and the treatment for his dry skin helped him look healthier. He became incredibly handsome with his olive skin, deep brown eyes and thick curly hair hinting at his father's Arab roots. The baby who some said would be a heartbreaker had turned into a heart melter, a toddler whose light healed the trauma of the previous 18 months and the nightmare we had lived through. His initial settling down problems were manageable, although my own physical health suffered.

As a result of post-traumatic stress, I began retaining fluid and my stomach became bloated practically overnight, as did my hands and legs. Migraines, constant fatigue and a feeling of sickness were daily occurrences and every day was uncomfortable. It took a year, many fruitless visits to the doctor and useless antacid treatments for me to take drastic action and eat nothing at all for 48 hours. The difference was almost miraculous, as during the last 12 hours aches came along then ebbed away. My joints became freer, eyes clearer and all that was left was a slight tightness in the base of my spine which wasn't at all uncomfortable. It was a remarkable feeling of rebirth.

Life became peaceful for a while and I began to think it was a good time to meet someone to have an adult relationship with. Internet dating has now largely taken over from the 'lonely hearts' pages in the newspapers but it was a solution for anyone lacking an obvious work or social outlet at that time. As there was limited opportunity to go out, it was to this medium I turned, which is how I met Matt.

Over the telephone, he sounded bright, cheerful and interesting. He was an unemployed musician who played in a band. This caught my attention as a love of live music or performance of most kinds was something we had in common. We spoke for some time about his musical aspirations, his friend who owned a recording studio and a babble of other things. At 30, he was four years younger than me. We set a date and place to meet. We spoke again on the telephone a few times before our date and seemed to get on quite well.

We had arranged to meet by the gates of Nottingham castle. Matt was wearing the green top and white jeans he had already told me about. He would have been easy enough to recognise in any case, as he was the only male there. We spent the rest of the evening in the outdoor seating area of the nearby Playhouse Theatre. As it was summer, the light was going to be with us for a few hours yet and it was a very warm evening. The evening went quickly and we laughed a lot. It was later than expected when we left as neither of us was in a hurry to get home.

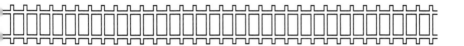

CHAPTER 17

Edmund had only been home for six months when a grant from the council to carry out renovation work on my house had been approved, but it meant moving out for six weeks because of the extensive work needed. A young couple I knew opened their home to us. Childless at that time, Andy and Jenny lived in a roomy, three-bedroom house. They had two cars, Andy's was a Volkswagen Golf but the smaller one was insured for any driver so it gave us the chance to travel further afield.

We had been with them in the weeks running up to Christmas and got back home with a few days to spare and no heating in the house. The fireplace in the dining room had been opened up to enable a real fire to be lit and another friend brought round a bag of coal, a house-warming present he had said. A short time after having lit it, the landing near the bathroom seemed quite smoky and upstairs in the house smelt strongly of bonfire. Edmund's bedroom, which was directly above the dining room, was full of smoke, which was pouring into his bedroom from behind the skirting board.

The builders had failed to check the flue, which had become porous over the years and was causing the problem. The fire had to be put out and the builder called. He refused to come back before

Christmas and all we had was a gas bottle heater that rocked when touched because one of the rubber feet was missing. Edmund's first Christmas at home, his third, was spent largely on our own, cold and really very dismally lonely. For some months, I'd been seeing Matt and the relationship seemed to be growing serious but he always had Christmas dinner with his parents so he spent the night with us and left the following morning. It was Christmas Day and we were on our own. Wrapping Edmund up warmly, I put him in the child seat on my bike and went for a ride.

The few nights spent back at home had been disappointing and my mood was gloomy so when Derek rang a couple of days after Christmas to say he needed to come and see me, I put him off. He could wait until after the New Year and at a time when Edmund was in bed because, as I pointed out, he was unlikely to be turning up with good news. That instinct was accurate.

Sitting on my sofa, the same one Edmund had been born on, was the first time Derek had been inside my house. I stood with my back to the window. Both of us were uncomfortable and I imagined he was inwardly cringing at the level of tidiness. The carpet in my dining room, which had come with the house, was threadbare and put down without an underlay because it was to be replaced once the newly renovated room had been decorated. From the middle of the wall to the floor there was new plaster, and an unsightly ridge ran around the middle of the room where the old plaster had been chopped away and replaced over the top of the old wallpaper which Matt and I had removed in the evenings when Edmund was asleep at Andy and Jenny's house. It looked a mess.

From his position on the sofa, Derek leaned forward, resting his forearms on his knees, and told me he had been offered a new job which he had accepted. It was in Australia. The whole world was collapsing again. It meant he, his new wife and her daughter, along with Terran and Holly, would be selling the house and moving overseas. Stunned, my ex-husband was subjected to a rapid firing of questions. When were they expecting to go? As soon as everything was 'sorted out' he said. Did Terran and Holly know? Yes, they'd been told, he said. He had wanted to tell me sooner in case one of them 'let slip' but I'd put him off from doing so. What were their thoughts? They were pretty keen and quite excited, he said. It sounded very strange. Were these children so enraptured by emigrating they would suddenly lose all perspective of the value of knowing their mother and brother?

Denny and Chris were out there. They would get to know them. Denny was Derek's younger brother, who had been living in Brisbane with his wife and two children for about eight years at that time. Chris, the eldest of all the Harrison siblings, had emigrated in the early 1970s with his first wife and young son. What if my children didn't like it? Then they would all come back, Derek said. What if just one of them wanted to come back? There were very many questions to be asked and answered. He said they would all still come back.

Pointing out the unfairness of the burden to put on young children, I tried to talk my ex-husband into agreeing that in the event of one child being unhappy, they would be welcome to live with me rather than disrupting the happy child for the sake of the one wishing to return. He agreed to that but Derek was, in fact, in a position to agree to anything because the reality would have been very far removed. What if they didn't want to go or one wanted to but not the other? Those answers were fairly similar to the previous ones but he again insisted on Terran and Holly's eagerness to make the change.

What about the pets? What would they do with the cat? Derek hadn't thought that far ahead but I was desperately trying to make sense of the shock, clutching at all means and any to stop anything else precious from changing when everything was finally, after two years, starting to settle into a new kind of normal. Katie I would have back. She came to us as a kitten when Terran had just passed his second birthday. It would be better for the children to know where the now elderly cat was. As few changes as possible at a time, that was how I preferred life. It was such an autistic response and so very typical to need to maintain as much consistency as possible.

Too shocked to know how to respond adequately, I told Derek I wouldn't sign anything. Edmund had been home for nine months after a very long fight. I wasn't going to give my children away. A huge part of the motivation to bring Edmund home was so he could know his brother and sister. Just as life was starting to pull together, it was again falling apart.

Matt came round shortly after Derek left. Removing his motorcycle helmet and gloves he asked, "Well? What happened?" He already knew about the visit. "He got a new job," I said. "How far away?" He guessed straight away when I said, "How far away can you get?" Telling him as much as I could remember, there was little else to say, but at bedtime I cried until the early hours of the morning.

As a result of Edmund's injury, losing contact with Terran and Holly had been a growing prospect from the time we had left the mother and baby home. After that first telephone call to their father, when Ed was placed with the foster carers, it was obvious that the freedom of unsupervised days out and weekend visits wouldn't simply carry on as they used to. A large motivating factor, if an additional one was ever needed, was the impact their brother's adoption would have had on the relationships with my two older children. Having endured the unreal settings of hospital, St Joseph's and shame of the contact centre, even I foresaw the problems which would have occurred should my younger son have been taken away.

But the miracle happened and Edmund came home. The four of us enjoyed as much family time together as circumstances permitted. Watching them having fun without suffering the scrutiny of hostile and suspicious eyes remained novel and hadn't become so commonplace as to be taken for granted.

Now we had to build more memories, share happy times before Terran and Holly left for their new life. I wondered how long we had together before they went.

The summer before they left, the children were staying with me for the weekend. As we drove away from their house, Holly shrieked, "Oh no!" very dramatically, as seven-year-olds often do. She went on to say, "It's our school summer fair today and I can't go." I asked her why not and she said, "Because we're with you." "Then I'll take you," I said. So we went. They were each given a small amount of money to spend and allowed to wander around a little but not out of eyesight.

I mingled somewhat awkwardly with people who had once crossed the road to avoid me shortly after I left home. Men, it often seemed, when marriages broke down, abandoned their wives; women 'walked out on their kids'. Other parents were warm and friendly, less judgmental. Holly had her face painted, sometimes shyly spoke to the school friends she met and we left. On the drive home, we passed farmland, fields with horses and a litter-covered hill in the background. Terran called out, "Oh, please can we go to Cardboard Hill?" I knew straight away how it had come by its name but had never known until that point why there was always so much litter up there.

They were all playing. It was one of those rare moments when life seemed total, complete, where peace added perfection to a beautiful day. Not only was summer well underway and the sun hot, but all three of them were enjoying being alive and having fun. Terran and Holly kept bouncing past as they dry-sledged to the foot of the hill on their cardboard sheets. At the bottom of the hill, Eddy was dragging an enormous sheet of cardboard around behind him. If it had been possible to have eaten, drunk and bathed in that moment, I would have infused every sense and feeling from the light breeze to the heat of the sun and sound of children, my children, laughing. It was a scene that would have been unimaginable a year earlier, even less.

Time didn't matter. Not having to be back within a given timeframe for anyone or any reason added pleasure to the peaceful surroundings. We were the only ones there. Even the view of the motorway in the distant left-hand frame of the image seemed to enhance the moment. I sat to one side, slightly more than halfway up the hill and against a hedgerow, comfortably out of the way. Rolling myself a cigarette, I watched them. Nothing was as important as that moment in time. Not too many minutes earlier, I too had been dry-sledging down the hill but wearing shorts meant there was no protection between my legs and the lumpy grass. I'd held Eddy tightly between my outstretched legs but our combined body weight kept pushing us off the sheet of cardboard. My buttocks were already stinging from the grazes.

Reflecting on everything over the three years since leaving Derek, life was so very different and almost unrecognisable from the one back then. White clouds drifted across the sky that afternoon, taking with them memories, like film shorts replaying before fading into the distance. Was it really only three years?

Maybe that was where perfect peace came from. Not that any conflict, hurt, pain, illness or other disturbance was absent but that a lull in the middle of it all could be found. How good it would have been to have watched them play forever but time was running short. Soon they would be gone, to Australia and their new life. Calling them all together, we went home.

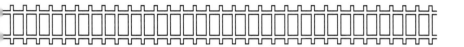

CHAPTER 18

The bedtime routine was always the same, the one we had from Edmund's birth. Holly and Edmund went in the bath together. They played, after a fashion; Eddy was an adept teaser and would do everything he could to make his big sister squeal, which made him repeat whatever action had caused her piercing reaction. Occasionally, the memory of the bath they'd had that December evening over three years earlier bobbed around among the bubbles as they played in the water. It was such an ordinary sight; bathing children was an activity enacted across the world and one which is so taken for granted by parents everywhere but I was grateful for those times. The day to day routines that took place were when I appreciated how fortunate they were to be together most of all.

The school fair and Cardboard Hill adventure had been some ten months earlier. This was a different bath time and we went through the same pattern of bathing the middle and youngest children together and having many cuddles and stories before Edmund's bedtime. It gave precious peace from a toddler's demands to enjoy my two older children. Once he was in bed, attention turned to my daughter. At that time, Holly slept in my bed and the two boys had the second bedroom. We cuddled and chatted as I settled her down for the night, in that most normal and familiar way everyone was comfortable with. Time meandered slowly as everything became a memory to tuck away in a secret place for the hurting times to come.

It had been a hot, busy day that started in the morning when I collected the children from their grandparents' house. I'd borrowed Andy and Jenny's car and drove the three children to Nottingham. We met up with my brother and David took photographs of us with my camera. I had gifts ready for them, including a razor for Terran, ready for the time he started shaving. At almost 14, it would have been something ahead, although not too far. He wanted a new watch, which I bought, as the strap on the one he wore was broken and held together with superglue.

For Holly, I bought a little necklace in silver. It had two chains and the pendant was a divided heart that said 'together' on one side and 'forever' on the other. I gave her the choice of which half she wanted and kept the other myself so she would know that however many miles there were between us, we would be together, forever. Around her neck was a round, clear plastic purse and she asked for some money. We had sat down at an open plan café in one of the city's shopping centres. She disappeared off to buy something to eat and came back with a plateful of doughnuts, one for each of us, including her uncle David. Holly forgot to take the purse with her so I kept it. The change and receipt are still there.

Holly was more than likely asleep before I reached the bottom stair. Something was on the television and I sat on the sofa with Terran to watch whatever it was distracting us from the inevitable pain the other two children seemed oblivious to. He kept holding my hand. "Will you be all right?" my big boy asked. "Yes," I replied, "I'll cry for as long as I have to, then I'll stop." There was no need to add anything else to either the question or its answer. We both could have enjoyed whatever was on the television but we weren't really watching. Maybe we were silently wondering whether that evening could have been spent doing something less ordinary.

Deep in thought, I would occasionally go outside for a cigarette, feeling guilty at leaving my son even for a few minutes. He asked again, "Will you be all right?" My reply remained the same. "Yes," I replied, "I'll cry for as long as I have to, then I'll stop." It would be their last night with me and there were no tears, just a dance between a dangling calm in the air and a clammy hand gripping my stomach.

There were no tears the following morning either, when Andy came to fetch us all, me and my three children. He had agreed to drive us on our last journey together. My former father-in-law, Harry, was leaning on the gate, waiting for us, as the car stopped in front of the house. He looked ill. He was dying of leukaemia but looked barely alive as he stood there.

The little boy remained in the car. Edmund was staying with me, the child it looked as though would be taken was left and the two I'd thought would always be there had already vanished into their grandparents' house without even looking around or waving goodbye. I watched, silently, as Holly laughed and ran in to show whoever would care the gift I'd bought the day before. I saw the back of her head and her blonde hair. I remembered how it had been spread across the pillow next to mine the night before and how I'd stroked through it before I went to sleep. Tomorrow they would be on an aeroplane, on a flight that would change everybody's lives.

There were still no tears. Andy drove us back. Before going home, he took me to another friend's house. She was a hairdresser and bridal gown designer, excellent actress and had a home hair salon. That morning she was going to cut my hair in some kind of symbolic gesture which made sense to me at the time. It was to represent grief and loss, powerlessness and despair. Sometimes a change in outward appearance represents a deeper meaning that extends beyond words.

I felt like a freak, a feeling which continued all day and was exacerbated by being a guest at the dedication of the baby son of someone in my circle. Almost no one in that group had children as most were in their early 20s. In itself, this was isolating because it was naturally hard for anyone to identify with the loss of children, or being at a social event and in sole charge of a three-and-a-half-year-old, which was Ed's age at that time.

Looking at the newly dedicated baby, surrounded by his family, drew my thoughts to Terran and Holly. How were they spending their last full day in England? I imagined eight-year-old Holly to be animated and cute, entertaining everyone with her pertinent and amusing observations. Terran was almost 14 and his voice was yet to break. He was, no doubt, lost somewhere in his own thoughts, his own world. He had always been a very self-contained boy. When busy, it was easy to absorb him in a task but he always seemed to start out from the point of frustrated boredom.

My first child, blond, wide-eyed and intelligent, had a vocabulary advanced for his age. Being the first grandchild on my side of the family and only the second baby amongst my friends, there were few positive role models to follow. My own childhood had been largely traumatic and I was exceptionally aware of how to be an awful parent, but did I know how to be a good one? Looking around the families I knew, the ones whom I perceived to be decent parents, all seemed to be from a different social class altogether and much wealthier. They were the ones I sought to emulate.

Throughout my pregnancy with him, I read books on child development and was fascinated by those on pregnancy and childbirth and especially pictures showing the growth of an unborn child at advancing weeks of gestation. I'd hoped for a boy. When he was born, he was given to me and I held him; he had horseshoe-shaped red marks on his cheeks from the forceps delivery and developed swellings on his head from the birth, which disappeared after a few weeks. There was no gush of emotion or instant bonding but he was fascinating. We grew and learned together. The ultimate creativity of a first baby is to turn ordinary people into parents.

It simply seemed like a good idea to enjoy being a parent and get as much out of this little life I'd been blessed with. In many ways, it was quite easy as I learned how to take a lead from Terran. His interests and the way he interacted with them were, looking back many years later, typical of an autistic personality. He was interesting. My parental view of him was quite objective and anthropological. He had access to a variety of experiences such as weekly swimming, a toddler group and visiting my grandparents. I have few memories of Terran ever playing with anyone his own age. Years later he would admit to never really liking children.

Terran liked books and learned his favourite ones by heart. This was also a good excuse for a cuddle. He would climb on to my lap. Lifting his shirt, he would say, "Tickle my back" before we had the story. At the library, he would find his own books, which is when his particular interests became obvious. He went through phases: crocodiles and alligators; heavy machinery; spiders; snakes; dinosaurs; spaceships and space travel; farming. He chose to his borrowing limit bar one, which I chose, insisting that at least one was a story book. At the point of leaving for Australia, he was painting miniature fantasy figures to the most minute of details. Eyeballs on the characters were no bigger than pinheads, yet he would paint thin red lines on to the irises and infill buttonholes and buckles to add definition and depth. His collection of paintbrushes included those only one bristle thick. His fine motor skills had been unusually good.

Oh Holly. My beautiful little girl was delivered after a very short labour. She looked very much like Terran had, although with slightly longer hair. I held her for the entire time between getting on to the hospital ward until visiting time when Derek brought Terran to see his new baby sister. Short for his age, he strode into the room we were in, swinging his shoulders and looking very important in jeans and a grey sweatshirt. He sat next to me, on Holly's side of the bed, crossed his legs, looked down at his new sister and said, "She's got a cute nose."

The pain and grief was crushing. It was a lonely, empty feeling. Memories from the past 18 or so months played in the background. Just as it had been when Edmund was in care, I'd made every visit from them count. We had been on holiday to Portsmouth, to stay with some friends, Penny and Bill. I reflected on that time and the trip to the Isle of Wight and how Edmund had run around naked, digging holes in the sand; how Holly had wandered off collecting shells in a bucket; how we threw our leftover supper for the seagulls to catch.

I took endless photographs. The pictures were of happy children; pictures of Penny and Bill's eldest son, soaking Holly with a hosepipe in their garden. It was fun, the way childhood ought to be. I took photographs from the time we took my dad to The National Film Museum. I remembered the time I drove the children on a two-hour round trip to an ice cream factory, just to buy ice cream.

Had I done enough, given enough, for them to remember me fondly and with love? Was it enough to last a lifetime? I had no idea when it would be possible to ever see them again. I was a single parent, jobless. It would need a massive turn of luck or a miracle to get to Australia to see them.

Had it not been for the small boy dependent on me, it would have been easy to have given up. Too much had happened over the three and a half years and too many battles fought and won for that to even be considered a possibility. Human beings are much stronger than they sometimes give themselves credit for and it took many years for me to realise I was one of those people.

The tears came in waves. As with any kind of grief, they came like the stealthiest thief, in ordinary moments, at stressful times, in public and in private. I fell into prolonged weeping sessions. Many times I wondered what I'd done to deserve so much pain. Had I been such a dreadful person, such a bad mother? It was the way I'd told Terran, crying for as long as I had to, then I stopped. I had to live. I had to hope.

I was halfway through a two-year college course when Terran and Holly left. I'd enrolled on a media course a few months after learning of the move to Australia in an attempt to increase my employability. It would help me to save for a trip to visit the children, as remote a possibility as it seemed. I used the desktop publishing skills I was acquiring to write what I hoped were funny and interesting letters which were sent to them every week. Edmund was happy in the college nursery and the cycle ride from home helped with my grief.

PART 2 - A NEW JOURNEY

CHAPTER 19

Edmund was about six weeks short of turning five when he started school. He had a place in a school a short walk up the road from where we lived. In common with any new starter, he had a new coat, uniform and lunch box. He looked very smart and was far taller than any of the other new starters. I left him in the classroom with his new teacher and went home. If there had been any idea of what was to follow, I would have stayed with him, but as with most parents of children his age, I expected Eddy to settle in fairly effortlessly.

This wasn't to be the case. Parents began to complain about his behaviour. His teacher was reporting Edmund was disruptive. Children in Ed's class told their parents about it. Playground conversations with other parents had always been awkward from the time Terran had started nursery school, but here at this school they were non-existent. Only one other parent ever spoke to me.

To begin with, it was suggested Edmund come home for lunch. Then he was put on a reduced timetable, only attending in the mornings. His class teacher rewarded every positive action with a smiley face sticker. Even sitting on a chair, sitting in the quiet corner or at a table were rewarded with stickers and his blue sweatshirt was covered in them by the time he left school. Nothing worked. He kept trying to escape from school. There were many, many occasions when staff had to pull him off the school gates because he tried to climb them to get out.

He regularly threw chairs across the room and attacked classroom assistants. He once stabbed one in the hand with a fork. He would lash out at anyone who challenged him and his language was foul, swearing and screaming abuse at everyone. The headmaster, at the end of one school day, rolled back his shirt sleeve and showed me the teeth marks my son had left when he bit him. I had no idea what to say but my answer was quick when his class teacher asked how I coped with him at home. "He doesn't do this at home," I said. This wasn't to last and soon the behaviour that had started at school came home.

Edmund was at his first school for one term and four days before I was told not to take him back. He was five years and three months old and permanently excluded from school. I heard the news in a telephone call from them shortly before lunchtime. I'd been working in the offices of a small but growing IT company. I hated it but hoped it would help to pay for the flight to Australia I longed to take to see Terran and Holly. The telephone call changed everything. I left the job without handing in my notice. It would be many years before I was able to work again.

I got a referral to Child and Adolescent Mental Health Services (CAMHs). We saw two people on that and subsequent visits but the initial interview set a precedent for other visits to other professionals across two counties. They asked questions such as, "Who is at home?" Puzzled, I said, "Nobody, we're here." I'd taken their question totally literally. Their question was re-phrased. "Who lives at home?" This made much more sense. "Just me and Edmund," I answered. The female of the pair looked at me. Tipping her head to one side, she softly said words that would also be repeated during interviews in different settings over the coming years. "It's not easy bringing up a child on your own, is it?" It was a confusing question with an underlying inference of parental incompetence. Of course it wasn't easy, raising children rarely was, regardless of whether they had one resident parent or two.

Terran had experienced difficulties at school at a similar age and older. I brought this into the equation, saying he had been in a two-parent family at that age. The common denominator was me. Maybe I was just a bad parent, but my sons had both been fine until they started school, so believing I was to blame made no sense. Terran's behaviour had, it was true, been very similar but not as extreme as his younger half-brother's and he had never been violent at home. Yes, he would roll around on the floor, run out of the classroom, throw chairs across the room and turn tables over the way Edmund had but he never attacked anyone. At school he was seen as a naughty boy, but at home he had always been well behaved. He was never really demanding of my time. It never struck me as unusual that he seemed to live in his own world. Why would it? I'd been the same.

By this time, Eddy was becoming increasingly challenging. I learned, years later, that he was experiencing meltdowns. At the time, they seemed like tantrums. He would have four or five every day, whether we were out in public or at home. He would also wake up in the night with endless screaming. I was always on edge and always tired. For what seemed like no reason at all, he would swear at me or shout, "I hate you, I hate you," while threatening to hit me with a cricket or baseball bat. These were snatched off him and thrown away. He would pick up dining chairs, throw them across the room, smashing them.

His night-time meltdowns were always around 2.30am and it would take over an hour to get him back to sleep. One night, he came into my bedroom while Matt was staying over. He held a hammer above Matt's head. "I'm going to kill you," he said. I leapt out of bed and pulled the hammer from his hands. Matt never moved and I was left on my own to try and settle the screaming boy back into his room. My patience often wore thin.

Another night, when I was at home on my own, Edmund came into the bedroom. He was dressed, wearing a coat and had two carrier bags with him. He must have been up and awake for quite a long time. He was standing at the foot of the bed. "I'm leaving home," he said. Foggy with sleep, I asked him why. "I don't know," was his answer. "All right," I replied. At least he wasn't screaming at this point. He left the room and I heard him go downstairs. Thinking he was just going to play, I let him.

From my bed, I could hear the back door repeatedly opening and closing. Then everything went quiet. I went down to check on him. He was gone. I ran back upstairs and got dressed as quickly as possible. Outside, I looked up and down the street, then round the corner near the house. There was no sign of him and there was no way of knowing which direction he would have walked in. If he came home he would find the house empty and be afraid.

I called the police. "My little boy has run away," I said. "How old is he, madam?" I said he was five but about as tall as a seven- or eight-year-old. "And what was he wearing?" they asked. It was only when I heard myself ask the counter question of, "How many five-year-olds do you think are walking around at 3 o'clock in the morning?" that it hit me. I started to cry. He was a little boy and something was troubling him. A moment later, and while I was still on the telephone, the operator told me they thought they'd found him. A passing police car had seen him and picked him up a mile away from home. The carrier bags he had with him contained pyjamas and his favourite teddy bear. The house keys were always kept out of reach after that.

He had a two-week, full-time assessment with the Child and Adolescent Mental Health team. A taxi collected him in the morning and returned him later in the day. During that time his behaviour was impeccable and the assessors saw nothing of the violence and awful language that had started in school. This was further confirmation of inadequate parenting. Nobody ever made the correlation between starting school and the beginning of the aggression. Edmund had become a very disturbed little boy. I had no idea how to help him. Whatever it was, we were in it together and I did everything to try and help him.

When he was in hospital, I was told he could be left with brain damage that may not show up until he was older, but my suggestion this may have had something to do with Edmund's explosive behaviour was discounted. We saw more professionals at other clinics but the focus was always on me. I was asked about my own childhood, which had been unhappy, and I was deeply probed about it. It was very uncomfortable to have ghosts dug up over times I was by then reconciled with.

Edmund spent the remainder of what should have been his second term at school at home with me. This created difficulties for two reasons. The first was his unpredictable behaviour, which created an enormous amount of stress, and the second was the questioning we got when we were out. He was often asked why he wasn't at school. There was never an easy answer and we would both lie. Edmund would say he had an inset day and I would say he had a doctor's appointment. They were humiliating times but never as awful as the public meltdowns he had, although these began later and slowly.

Thinking he would function better in a smaller school, I managed to enrol Ed in a small Christian school in a nearby village. It was fee paying and there was no way I could afford it but children were taken on in these circumstances if a parent would help out in the classroom. I was happy to volunteer and would spend one day a week there. There were only two classrooms and 22 children on the register between the ages of five and 11. The uniform was very strict. The boys wore grey shorts and the girls wore skirts or pinafores. Shirts were formal and children had to learn how to fasten a tie. Boys had caps and girls wore straw hats.

Given the layout and rural setting of the school, there was a distinct reminder of tradition and old English village life, which was why many parents chose to educate their children there. It was very much like home education in formal surroundings. There was something very comforting about it. Set on the main road of the village, it backed on to open fields and was adjacent to a small children's park. At break time, the children would often stand on the school railings to get a better view of passing horses and farm machinery.

The infant school teacher lived quite close and she would pick Eddy up in the morning with her own three children. My little boy seemed to settle in well. I enjoyed my one day a week, especially during World Book Day that year, when all the children dressed as favourite characters from books. I pretended to be Lois Lane, Clark Kent's colleague in the *Superman* stories and interviewed all the infant school aged children. That weekend, I wrote it up into a story and laid it out in the style of a front page news story. On the Monday, I took it into school, photocopied it into an A5 size and sold copies to parents. It was very popular as it mentioned every single character the children had dressed as.

The school was very heavily overseen by the rector of the village church and his wife. Reverend and Mrs Gooding had lived and worked in the area for many years and had been frequent visitors to the Christian conference centre I'd worked at when Terran was a toddler. I never found out why but Mrs Gooding took a dislike to my son. His behaviour, I was told, was very good but he was somehow different from the other children. He even once won a certificate for good behaviour, which was presented to him by the headmistress at the end of term. Walking off the stage, holding his certificate against his chest, Mrs Gooding asked to look at it. Handing it over to her, she said, "You don't deserve this," and tore it up in front of parents and pupils.

The children had been preparing for a whole school event at the parish church for a number of weeks and each child had an individual part. I sat with the other families, trying to catch sight of my son but couldn't see him. It was dark, as ancient churches often are, and all the children were dressed in uniform, but surely I should be able to recognise my own son? Afterwards, I went into a room at the back of the church and saw him, sitting on his own, playing with a little hand-held game. Bewildered, I asked if he was all right. He was very quiet. A nearby member of staff told me Mrs Gooding had prevented him from taking part. I was furious and hurt. It didn't seem either a kind or Christian action to take against a five-year-old boy.

Edmund was there for one term, leading up to the long summer break, when the school broke down. Both teachers left. The infant teacher founded another independent school in another village and Edmund, who had always liked his teacher, was enrolled to start the following September. He was almost six.

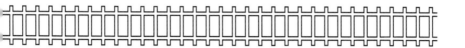

CHAPTER 20

With another new start ahead of Edmund, despite this being his third school in a year, I felt confident it would be a good move. He liked his teacher. Mrs Marks had been the first person to mention Edmund displayed traits of Asperger's syndrome. I had no idea what this was. She must have said it was a form of autism because I seemed to have always known the two conditions were linked. When asked about her reasons for thinking Ed was autistic, she told me children often took things literally and gave me an example from a time the school went on a woodland walk. She had said they were going to walk through the trees and Eddy had been running up to and bumping into them, saying, "Look, I can't walk through the trees."

Looking for work opportunities, I enrolled on a government sponsored training course. It was very basic but it offered a work placement, paid childcare and a small amount of money on top of my Social Security benefits. The young friends who often had Ed overnight agreed to look after him for the money I was given.

Although work placements were usually found by the training centre, their options looked uninteresting so I found one of my own. I thought long about the area which, given the choice of anything in the world, would be ideal for me. Having spent some time on work experience at Nottingham Playhouse while I was at college, I telephoned them and asked for the African and Caribbean Arts producer who had supervised my time there. She had left and her role had been filled by two men, Paul and Stuart, as a job share.

Rosie, the receptionist on the stage door, put me through to Stuart. It was a long and inspiring conversation and they were very interested in providing the opportunity I was looking for. With Black History month approaching, I was sure to be helpful. We set up an interview time for me to go in and Stuart asked me to take in a CV, which I actually posted instead. There was one very important question that needed to be asked. Did it matter that I was white? No, Stuart explained that he too was white and he had taken the position at the Playhouse on the understanding that Paul, who was of black African descent, would job share with him. As it happened, my assistance proved to be invaluable.

I was working unpaid but committed to two days a week, providing I could leave in enough time to get home for when Edmund was dropped off from school. Paul and Stuart were out of the office more often than not and I would spend many hours on my own, dealing with any administrative jobs that came along. My office was little more than a wide corridor leading to the more private and larger office of the main stage producer. There were other desks in the office which were taken up by the in-house playwright and a younger woman whose job was unclear to me. Keeping a large notepad at my side, I made written records of any telephone calls that came in. There were many times I was able to answer queries and carry out tasks that came in, and although they were relatively mundane, they were time consuming and left the producers free to take on the more complex queries.

Playhouse staff, whether paid or not, were also able to book two free tickets to performances, including the annual pantomime. It was a fantastic opportunity to see live theatre, which was something I'd fallen in love with as a ten-year-old when our school went on a Saturday morning visit to the theatre I was suddenly working in.

That year, Paul and Stuart were planning an extensive African and Caribbean art exhibition over the three floors of Playhouse foyers. They gave me the task of writing labels for all the artworks. I was also asked to design, write and produce a printed programme to go with them. My desktop publishing skills had been picked up on by Stuart, who commissioned me for the job as they had no budget for one. I contacted all of the contributing artists to ask them to send in short biographies. Nobody responded so I interviewed all of them over the telephone instead.

Once it was ready to print and had met with approval from Paul and Stuart, I had to learn to use the photocopier to be able to print them. This took far longer than it should have because I didn't know the machine could be set to print both sides and undertook the entire task manually, which led to an awful lot of wasted paper. On the back of that, I was given a freelance paid task. This was to produce the programme for the African and Caribbean community pantomime, which was being shown in a local school. This meant more telephone interviews and photocopying.

One day, I was in the ground floor foyer, feeding letters through the franking machine and saw another member of staff sitting at a table, putting theatre tickets in envelopes. I asked the reason behind it and found they were often approached by charities for complimentary tickets for raffle prizes. This gave me the idea of having a competition, so I included one in the pantomime programme. Two children would win family tickets to a main stage production. It was work I was intensely proud of.

Neither Paul nor Stuart could drive so they got permission for me to drive the Playhouse van. After the end of Black History month,

I was needed to return artwork to various studios and workspaces around Nottingham. Never having had much contact with the African and Caribbean community, it was a fascinating window into another culture and everyone I met was very warm and open.

During this time, and shortly before Edmund turned six, Matt and I separated. He had been a key figure in our lives for over four years and I was heartbroken. Eddy saw him as a father and had been calling him Daddy from just after his second birthday. They had a warm and loving relationship, but ultimately the pressures created by Ed's outbursts at home were too much. He had grown distant and wouldn't discuss them at all. Edmund was also very fond of his granny, Matt's mother. She would often take him out for the day to visit her elderly father. I allowed Matt to see Edmund and he would come over one night a week to play with him, bathe him and put him to bed. I took the opportunity to go swimming.

After Christmas, the African and Caribbean Arts producers began rehearsals for an anti-racist play and I was offered another paid assignment, as tour organiser. It was to be staged at schools and youth clubs across three counties. Having no idea how to organise a tour, I learned as I went along. I rang the relevant local education authorities and had them send a list of comprehensive schools. I began making telephone calls. The importance of getting the name of an individual member of staff soon became obvious. It avoided phoning back to find the person at the end of the telephone had no idea about the play at all.

I also learned the fine art of doing a deal. If a youth club made an evening booking, I would contact the nearby schools and offer them a discount if they booked earlier on the same day. I also initiated a deal with larger schools to run for two consecutive days so all of the year group could take part.

Edmund was permanently excluded from school for the second time. As before, he had been there for one term and four days. He was six years old. A few days into the new term, he had exploded in a rage and had been throwing chairs across the classroom. He had also tried to run away. The teacher had been struggling to cope with low levels of aggressive behaviour from him for some time and had taken the decision to terminate his place for the safety of the other children. I was a couple of months into organising the touring play and had to complete the task I was being paid for. There was no other option than to take him with me when I couldn't find anyone to take him off my hands. He was always well behaved there and we'd sometimes stay to watch schools' productions or Thursday afternoon performances together.

At home, Edmund's behaviour escalated to a new level and it was made worse by having him at home full time. Whenever I took him out on day trips, his behaviour was excellent and we enjoyed each other's company, but the day to day living tasks were terrible. We couldn't walk the half a mile to the local supermarket. As soon as we got to the end of our street and on to the main road, Edmund would explode in a rage that seemed to come out of nowhere. He would run at me, screaming, "I hate you, I hate you, I'm going to kill you," and then try to push me into the road. More than being humiliating, which it was, it was terrifying. I was more concerned for his safety than mine. This would happen even when we were crossing the road. What if he had succeeded? I envisaged lying in the road, injured by a passing vehicle, looking at him standing on the pavement on his own.

There was no plan B. I was all he had. What would happen to him if anything happened to me? It wasn't just the attempts to push me into the road but the endless stream of bad language he shouted at me all the way to the shops. When we got to the supermarket, he would roll around on the floor screaming. Many times, he had to be dragged across the floor, out of the way of other shoppers. His outbursts were bad enough but there was no guarantee he wouldn't start pulling goods from the shelves to throw.

There were occasions when I feared he would run into the road or attack other shoppers. I would have to pull him to the ground. One thing I'd already learned was he found being held very tightly and rocked was calming. Ignoring the judgmental stares and muttering of passers-by, we would sit in the street and rock. I would speak quietly to him, saying, "I love you, I love you," over and over again. Emotionally, I was wafer thin and felt the same kind of degradation I'd had on the occasions my mum had beaten me.

Once, when I was on the ground holding and rocking Edmund, I saw a man approach. He could have easily done what other shoppers were doing and circled around us. He was getting closer. Was he going to offer to help in some way? He stepped right over us and looking back said, "He just needs a bloody good hiding." That was the last thing Edmund needed. To my shame, I'd tried and it just escalated his screaming and violence. I was desperate. Many times I wondered what kind of awful person I must have been to have deserved a child as terrible as this little boy, to have had such a difficult life.

The walk home was equally dreadful. It was common to be shouted at, pushed and threatened all the way into town. The half-mile walk could have been 30. Every step was an ordeal but Edmund was six and far too young to be left at home. It was on one of those walks home that breaking point happened. I was carrying the shopping. Edmund was a few steps behind and, as usual, hurling insults and bad language at me. I lost my temper completely. This had been building for months. Furious, I spun round and swung the shopping bags at him. He dodged them and carried on shouting.

We were just a few steps from the Social Services offices and I went inside. Edmund followed. Gathering as much self-control as was possible, I asked to see a social worker. "Take him off me, I can't cope with this anymore," I said and sat down in the waiting area, defeated, heartbroken and sobbing. At that moment, I thought he needed a decent mummy and daddy, a couple who would know what to do with him and give him a real home. Nobody would ever love him as much as I did but maybe he needed more.

A woman came out. She was somebody I recognised from the Family Support Centre Edmund had attended while he was in foster care. Leading us into a side room, she had a form in her hand. "Here, sign this." She spoke in a blunt and direct way. Edmund was standing quietly in the corner. The social worker continued, "But he won't go to a family. There are no families. He'll have to go into a home." She had called my bluff. My heart could not have broken more than it was that day. Nobody to love my son, nobody to play with him at bath time, cuddle him, give him the big tickles that made him laugh so much, or blow raspberries on his tummy. How could I do that to my own son, my own little boy? We were on our own. "Come on sweetheart, we're going home," I said.

I had to grow. I had to learn. I had to do something different.

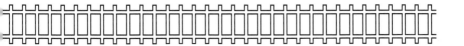

CHAPTER 21

Two things happened from the visit to the Social Services. One was we were given a social worker who began to look into daytime respite care to give me a break. The other was the growth of a strong belief it was my responsibility to develop strategies to manage Edmund's outbursts more effectively. Although physically and emotionally draining at times, it was only one aspect of the relationship we had. Outside of the challenging behaviour, our bond was incredibly strong and it was this I fell back on. He liked action and adventure and this was our starting point.

Thinking much bigger than before the visit to the Social Services office, I thought about the kind of activities Eddy enjoyed. The first obstacle to overcome was the walk to the supermarket, most of which was along a main road. Looking at how we could get there safely and knowing how he liked imaginative games and stories, I created a game.

Before we started out for the next shopping trip, I took Edmund outside. "Can you see this track where the pavement has been dug up?" I asked. He nodded. "Well, we're going to play a game," I said. He was engaged. Games were fun. "We're going to pretend this is a rope bridge," I told him. I pointed to the areas to either side of the narrow tarmac path. "The bridge goes over a canyon and way, way down below us is a river. In the river there are crocodiles. We have to walk very carefully along the rope bridge because if we wobble and fall off into the river, the crocodiles will eat us. Can you do that?" Ed nodded. "Shall I go first to make sure it's safe?" He nodded again. Putting one careful foot in front of another, we set off.

Eddy walked very carefully behind me. Now and again, I would stop, hold out my arms to steady myself and pretend to wobble. "Ooh, be careful." We walked very slowly to the end of the street and on to the main road. There were several side roads to cross so we would stop, flap our arms and pretend to fly to the other side. If we were ever the manufacturers of our own miracles, this was one of them. We got to the supermarket. Flying high on a kite of victory, my game was still underway. We were at the supermarket entrance and I stopped suddenly, turned around and said, "Follow me."

I started to run quite quickly, Edmund right behind, until we got to the canned food aisle. Gathering four little cardboard trays from underneath the cans, I dropped them on the floor. I put my feet in two of them and instructed Edmund to do the same. We carried out our shopping with little cardboard boxes on our feet. It was the second miracle and another victory. We were winning. The homeward journey took us back along the rope bridge over the canyon and well above the crocodile-infested river below. We were safe. If we were going to be stared at and judged by shoppers, it was far better, in my mind, to be having fun than trying to restrain an angry child. After that, every time we had to go into the town centre we would repeat the same game. Eventually, he settled down but we were building on the victories and shopping trips began to take on an element of fun.

The angry, explosive behaviour at home continued. This too required a strategy. Shouting back had only ever escalated his aggression. Standing back from it, I saw a frightened little boy. He didn't know what was troubling him either. This wasn't a child who hated me and neither did he want to kill me, despite his words. The next time he held a chair over his head and shouted, "I hate you, I hate you, I'm going to kill you," I stood very still, silent and a safe distance from him. "Well, I love you," I said very quietly. Repeating the words over and over again, I wished, willed and prayed for the love I had for him to pour into his heart and take his terror away. "I love you, I love you, I love you."

Fixing his gaze and never once looking at the chair, I walked slowly towards him. When close enough to remove it, I took it from him and put it down, somewhere behind me. "I love you. I love you. Come on, let's have a hug." Edmund crumpled into my arms, sobbing. "I'm sorry Mummy, I'm sorry. I love you Mummy." I held him tightly in the backwards hug that calmed him, rocking him until his tears stopped. "I love you too, sweetie. Let's just be friends. Come on, fetch a book, we'll have a story." He needed me to be bigger, braver and stronger than whatever was troubling him.

The strategies began to pay off. Life, along with our relationship, improved and the boy I knew before he started school was beginning to emerge once again.

The social worker introduced us to Mandy, a respite foster care worker looking for her first placement. It was a total disaster. Edmund had convinced himself the woman was going to kill him so he spent the entire day locked in the bathroom, refusing to come out. She called the police, which only added to his fear. A social worker from the Family Support Centre came round and after a considerable number of hours Edmund came out. Later on, I asked what had happened and all he said was, "She was fat and smelly, Mum."

The social worker found us another respite care placement and took us to visit her. Edmund was sold immediately. Kerry was 26 and single, slim and pretty. She lived in a tidy semi-detached house and loved sport. She worked as an instructor at a leisure centre and loved quad biking. She was even willing to have him stay overnight on occasions. They went swimming and for long walks. She took him quad biking and introduced him to friends and family. I got valuable rest and the release from endless stress helped enormously at home. Edmund was sleeping better and life was improving for both of us. The meltdowns and aggression were still present and would remain so for many years but he never had an outburst with Kerry.

As he was facing the remaining school year at home, the local authority found a home tutor, who would visit the house for two hours at a time, twice a week. I kept out of the way by decorating Eddy's bedroom. Once this was finished, I joined the gym at the local leisure centre and began working out. My cycling had tailed off a lot since he became too big to carry on the back of my bike but I would often take myself out on a ride while he was with Mrs Dixon. It was her job to try and maintain the basics of education with Edmund. On her days off, we would often take the day out. Sometimes we would meet my dad at a McDonald's in the city centre. Most of the time, Edmund was perfectly fine.

My father was very suspicious that the reports of his grandson's challenging behaviour were exaggerated until the day he witnessed it for himself. Edmund had taken a toy sword which had been entertaining him for some time. At some point, he decided he wanted ice cream, but as he had already had sweets, I said no. Immediately, Edmund flew into a rage, hurling bad language and threats at me, pushing and pulling at my clothes. Other customers were already staring and we decided to leave. Ed followed, hitting me with the sword and shouting abuse. We ignored him but this

THE JOURNEY OF AN AUTISTIC MOTHER

had no effect at all. Dad was non-judgmental and simply said, "I wouldn't have believed it if I hadn't seen it. I didn't realise he was this bad." Looking across at my father, I replied, "Dad, he's far worse than this."

When I could borrow the car from Andy and Jenny, we would drive out to somewhere different. Edmund always liked the journeys and being outdoors and was always a pleasure to be with. At other times, we would buy a day ticket that allowed us to travel on as many trains and buses around the county as we liked. Eddy loved the adventure element and the changing scenery we saw from train and bus windows. Even when the journey plan went wrong, it didn't matter as we had nobody to go home to. On days like those, I knew Edmund would go to bed a peaceful and contented boy.

Facts and statistics fascinated Ed and he would often come home from his second school desperate to tell me something fabulously exciting. The class had been learning about the Black Death, the plague that had spread across London in 1665. "Mum, guess what," he had said, "the plague wasn't caused by the rats. It was the fleas on rats." Not long after that day, there was an advertisement for the plague museum in the village of Eyam, a village in the Peak District National Park and famous for its outbreak of the plague in the mid-17th century. I decided to take him.

It was the first of the two Bank Holidays in May and the village was overrun with tourists. Pulling into the car park, we heard gunfire. Thinking it came from hunters in the surrounding woodland, I thought nothing of it and we went to the village museum. When we left, we noticed an event on at Eyam Hall which was in the village centre. A camp had been set up on a field at the back of the hall and people of all ages were in costumes typical of mid-17th century England. Men were making shot, the round bullets used in muskets, from molten lead poured into moulds.

An elderly man was showing a young tourist how to make wooden spoons on a lathe. Children, also in costume, were playing together and play fighting with one or two of the older men. Everything about it fascinated us.

Edmund liked weaponry and military equipment and we spoke to a few of the musketeers. It was then we found out what the gunfire we had heard earlier actually was: it was a musket-firing demonstration put on by the group. Everything looked family orientated and those we spoke to were friendly. Seeing it as an ideal opportunity to get away for weekends, make friends and meet people, we asked about joining and arranged to go away with the group at the end of that month.

Mum had previously offered me a sum of money to take Edmund away on holiday. Knowing how his behaviour affected him, I declined. If anything, I thought we would potentially be more isolated than we already were. Neither of us had any real friends. Edmund was far more challenging than other children of his age and maintaining friendships became embarrassing. The effort demanded too much from me. My self-esteem was still very low.

After our weekend with the re-enactment group, I rang Mum and asked if her offer of holiday money was still open. It was enough to order a reproduction 17th century soldiers' tent that was far bigger than we really needed but there was room to stand up in and space to store our equipment. After that, we spent four or five weekends away with the group, trying to fit in and make friends. It was worth it for the experience of camping in some incredibly beautiful and historical sites across the country. Because we had an authentic tent, we were regularly sleeping inside the confines of castle walls. There was no safer place to leave Edmund sleeping at night while I sat around the campfire with the other re-enactors.

The saying 'it takes a village to raise a child' was no truer than in that group. Over a few seasons, we began to find a place. Edmund's occasional outbursts were generally confined within our relationship and he could make life very difficult. He was clearly the least well-behaved child in the group and would often push me to the edge of my patience. It was the intervention of two older members, Des and Pete, who worked another miracle. The two men were in charge of a small cannon called a falconet. Des, in particular, had an authority about him that Edmund respected. A former prison officer, he was tolerant and patient.

At one event, when Edmund was around eight, Des and Pete asked if Ed would like to help them 'on the gun'. They made the role sound very important. Edmund was delighted. He had always had a liking for older people and was happy to be involved. He was given a heavy wooden bucket and told to collect fresh grass, which was needed for the firing displays. It had to be pushed down the barrel of the gun and dry grass would have caught fire. It was a genius move and the child took his job very seriously, listening closely to instructions given by the older men.

When he misbehaved, I would threaten to report him to Des and Pete and ask them not to allow him to work on the gun. When the threat failed, I would indeed speak to his friends, who would put a hand on either his shoulder or head. Both were very direct and always called him 'Boy'. Speaking to him in serious voices, they would say, "Now look here Boy, if you don't behave for your mum, you won't be working with us today. Do you understand?"

It never once failed and was so successful that at the group Christmas party, he was awarded with his own cut-down musket.

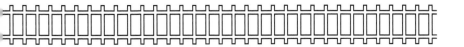

CHAPTER 22

Mrs Dixon, the home tutor, worked with Edmund until a new school was found. She was also to help the transition from home succeed. As his other school places had failed, it was thought a gradual introduction would help. For a few weeks, Mrs Dixon would collect Ed in her car and drive him to school, which was actually only walking distance from home. The plan after that was for me to walk him there. It clearly stressed him so I resorted to an adapted strategy, similar to the one we had used to get to the town centre.

This time, instead of walking along an imaginary rope bridge, we played I-spy. Edmund always won because his answers always referred to small details and most of these were on cars. For instance, his 'W' would have been wiper blade or wheel nut. It kept his mind occupied until we got to where we would meet his tutor.

This was his fourth infant school in the space of two years and one he never even got to attend full time. I was heading home from a long bike ride when my mobile phone rang. It was school. Edmund was in the throes of the worst school-based meltdown he had ever had and nobody knew what to do. When I got there, the police had been called and Edmund was climbing out of windows, running round the building and coming back in through the door. He had been screaming non-stop and throwing chairs and tables around his and other classrooms. The other children were terrified. He was seven and permanently excluded from his third school.

All through his school life, the local authority Schools Inclusion Officer had been working with us and had been present at the many meetings we had been called to attend. John Sinclair was a quietly spoken Scotsman who worked very hard to secure an education for my son and it had been at his insistence that Edmund be given a home tutor rather than attend a Pupil Referral Unit. It was very rare for a child as young as Ed to be permanently excluded from one school, let alone three, and the others at the PRU would have been much older, many with criminal convictions and poor attendance. It would have made a very unsuitable environment for such a young child.

It was Mr Sinclair who found a new school for Edmund to begin his junior school years in and an appointment was made to visit. Holly House was a small school in the north of the county for children with emotional and behavioural problems. At one time, it would have been a village on the outskirts of the town and many older buildings still stood. The school was up a hill that began as a wide road that narrowed into a lane at the top. A farm was directly opposite the school gates. From the car park and many of the classrooms, there was a spectacular view across a valley and over the town itself. Regardless of any school ethos, it was in a fabulous location and had a sense of openness and freedom. We looked around the school and met many of the staff, who were all warm and friendly. The decent sized gym had a climbing wall that stretched across one of the longer sides. The woodwork teacher, who also taught pottery, became one of Edmund's favourite teachers. He was an older man with a strong but calm nature. It already felt like the perfect place for my son to thrive.

It was a school for children from the age of 7 to 14 with a residency block built on to the back. Most children spent one or two nights a week there and Edmund was to stay for just the one. Out of school activities included horse riding and visits to the local swimming pool in the town. Holly House had its own minibus and children were often taken on outings. Class sizes were small and although I was uncomfortable with him being at a special school, there were really no other options. Unlike the other schools, uniform and meals were provided. A taxi would be arranged to collect Edmund in the morning and bring him home in the evening.

The children were awarded points for good behaviour, which could be cashed in for shopping vouchers. When they wanted to buy anything, the children would choose something from a catalogue and staff would order then collect it for them. Ultimately, Ed would save his points to buy goods I'd refused to replace when he had broken them during meltdowns. Once he began to realise the value of working and saving for special items, nothing ever got broken at home again. He even used his reward points to buy my birthday and Christmas gifts.

The greatest and most rewarding relationships Edmund built during his time at Holly House were with his taxi drivers, the first one being Rob. A sole operator in his early 40s, Rob was very overweight but made fun of his own very large stomach. He would often stop off on the way home from school to buy drive-through meals from McDonald's for himself and the boys in his taxi. Edmund would come home with funny stories of how Rob would steer the taxi with his stomach while he was eating. He would also bring back reports of misbehaviour of the other boys and how Rob would deal with these, including chasing and rugby tackling an absconder to the ground.

Occasionally another driver would collect Ed and another boy, Ben, who lived a few miles away and they too would be talked about at home. Edmund often said he liked to hear other people's stories and he would retell these at home. He also had a strong bond with Carole, Rob's partner. She took over the school run following Rob's sudden and unexpected death. It was the first funeral Edmund had ever been to and one that affected him deeply.

Very early on in his time at the school, it became very obvious there was an impressive continuity and consistency of care between staff, parents and the taxi drivers. Maybe it was helped by my own input. Perhaps it was the openness of the staff but communication between me and the school was the best we could have hoped for. If there was ever an issue at home, I would let school know. If I made a disciplinary decision, staff would respect it. In return I valued their decisions. I became a parent governor at the school, the only one they'd had for a number of years.

Edmund was possibly one of the most polite and well-behaved children in the school and, as I suspected, he had less of a behavioural issue and more of a reaction to his environment. His tolerance of violence towards staff from other children was low. He would often come home with stories of a child who had attacked a teacher. "It's not right, Mum. David hit Mrs Sharp today so I hit him. Children shouldn't hit teachers." Peer pressure must have been quietly condoned on this account as no one at school ever raised this as an issue with me. Life at Holly House was the best experience Edmund could have had and no move was ever made to reintroduce him to mainstream education.

When he was eight, he went through a prolonged phase of refusing to get dressed for school. The taxi would arrive at around the same time every morning to try and beat the traffic and I began to lose patience. One day I lost my temper completely and heard myself shout, "If you don't get dressed and ready for school, you'll go in your pyjamas." Edmund looked terrified and ran out of the house, still in his nightclothes. Too angry to chase him, I stuffed his school uniform into a carrier bag, along with his breakfast toast.

The taxi arrived. I grabbed the coat, shoes and carrier bag. Carole was outside in the taxi when I went outside. Pulling the door open, I said, "Here's his coat, here are his shoes, these are his clothes. His breakfast is in the top of the carrier bag." I pointed to Edmund hiding around the corner. "Edmund is over there and don't bring him back until tonight." I went back in the house, shaking with rage. I rang school to let them know what to expect when Edmund's taxi arrived. They thought it was hilariously funny and teased Eddy about it all day. The next day, still amused, they asked where his pyjamas were. There was never an issue getting ready for school after that.

Ed was no fan of sleeping at school and although he usually only made low-level complaints about it, he once decided to run away. He and Ben, the boy he shared a taxi with, got out of the car one morning and immediately headed for the field at the back of the school. A member of staff contacted me and the police were called. I rang work and took the day off to wait for news. An officer from the local police station came to take a statement from me while Chesterfield police put out a missing person's alert. Both boys returned, tired, hungry and thirsty at the end of the school day. I was called immediately. I insisted he stay over at school as usual but wasn't to go to the planned horse riding lesson, which was an activity he really enjoyed. It was the only time he ran away from school.

Holly House always welcomed parental involvement, which I appreciated enormously. I attended a few events, mainly sports days which were held at a playing field in the town centre. Edmund was very similar to Terran in as much as he was ambivalent towards competitive events. Whilst other children would race along, my boys showed no interest at all. It was something barely worth making an issue of, even when I'd taken time off work to be there. It was quite amusing to turn up to watch the afternoon sports and see Edmund finishing a race with another boy at a walking pace and eating a packet of crisps.

There were other events I took part in and one of those was a pirate themed day, where children and staff dressed in costumes. Some boys had shop-bought outfits but I adapted clothing from Ed's re-enactment kit and he looked amazing. The gym was used for an afternoon of piratical fun and games that most enjoyed. My son was quite happy to be there but wouldn't join in with the games, instead choosing to occupy himself at the edge of the room.

He liked dressing up and would often be very creative, which was the case when the school had a non-uniform day to raise money for charity. He was ten at the time and only a few inches shorter than me. He decided to go, he said, as a girl. The night before, I sorted out a black leather skirt and boned black velvet vest, which he wore with fishnet hold-up stockings. Over the top of everything, he had on a red leather motorcycle jacket. I even found a wig for him which I'd bought but never worn. His feet were already far larger than mine so he had to wear school shoes. When he put everything on, I said, "Eddy, you look gorgeous," and we both laughed. When he came home that evening, he said a few truck drivers on the motorway had winked at him so he had blown kisses at them.

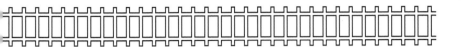

CHAPTER 23

The radio had always been a constant in family life and over the years I'd won a few interesting and rewarding listener competitions. Once I won a family ticket to see Disney on Ice. The condition was we had to go on the radio station's breakfast show the following morning to talk about it. The tour round the radio and TV station afterwards was far more interesting and fun than Disney on Ice had been. On another occasion, I won a weekend break for two in a five-star London hotel, which led to being invited to join the breakfast show to read the traffic and travel news live on air. Despite the constantly challenging behaviour, Edmund and I had a strong bond and we enjoyed having fun together.

A month or two after the traffic and travel news radio adventure, there was another competition, called 'Get Home for Christmas with Simply Red' and was promoting the new album by the band Simply Red. The aim was to reunite people over the festive season with loved ones who lived overseas. The prize was two return plane tickets to anywhere in the world. It sounded interesting but I paid it little attention. The second time I heard it, I thought 'I'm going to win that'. It was a regional radio station that joined up with sister stations at night to broadcast nationally.

Edmund was ten and we both had passports in the event of ever having to make an emergency trip to Australia. If either Terran or Holly had an accident or serious illness, I would have wanted to go.

Entrants had to write in or email the story of who they would visit, how they were related, which country they lived in and why they wanted to go. The intention was to reward the winner with a long-haul flight. I told our story, the one of how two of my children had gone to live in Australia with their father. I told of my heartbreak and of my love for them. I told of them going from being 7 and 13 to 15 and 20 and had grown from children to young adults without me. I told how it was over six and a half years since we had seen each other and their ten-year-old brother had no memory of them. I told my story and sent the email.

We made the shortlist of three and the finalists had their stories published on the radio station website. Each entrant was interviewed over the telephone, live on air, and the finalists were voted for by the public. My story won 95% of the internet votes. We were going to Australia.

I'd never flown anywhere and we were going to see my children. It was surreal. In the years since they left, I'd often imagined that first meeting, when I got off the aeroplane to meet them. Would I recognise them? Would we fall into each other's arms and cry? A few weeks after winning the competition, I would find out. We had to buy suitcases and go Christmas shopping. Both of my parents gave me money for things we needed for the flight and gave me presents to take over for the children. The space they took up in the suitcases left plenty of room for the ones I would bring home. I saw a cuddly Christmas reindeer in the local supermarket and bought it for Holly. I carried it all the way to Australia. It was for my daughter.

It took about 11 hours to get to Narita airport in Tokyo and then we had another nine-hour wait for our connecting flight. Too concerned about getting lost if we went outside, we spent the entire time at the airport. Edmund and I were both very tired so I booked us into a rest room for a shower and short sleep before continuing our flight. Another long flight lay ahead and both Eddy and I were living in the moment, barely speaking to each other. Sometimes we would try to doze on the aeroplane but it was all too strange for that to happen. I would, as I'd done on the first plane, take regular walks between watching films and following the flight on the TV in the back of the headrest of the seat in front.

Then, through the windows of the aeroplane, we started to see land. We could see houses, rivers, trees and roads. Soon we would be landing. This was Australia. Anticipation and anxiety rose inside me in waves. Never had I thought this moment would happen. I had often wished it would. Not really knowing what to do, Edmund and I followed the instructions given to us at every gate and inspection point we passed through. The wait at the final checkpoint seemed endless.

The children were waiting just beyond the barrier. I recognised them instantly, even though it had been years since they'd sent a photograph. They looked so much like their father's younger brother and sister. Still dazed and tired by the long flight, Eddy and I walked up to them. "We got here," I said. Terran looked at me. At 20, he was much shorter than I'd imagined. He spoke, "You're so little." Looking at his younger brother, he said, "And you're so big." The ten-year-old was the same height as his sister. I turned to Holly. "This is for you," I said and handed over the Christmas reindeer. "I thought you might like it. I carried it all the way from home." She took it from me and gave me a hug. Terran then said, "Shall we go?" There were no tears, no waves of emotion. Over six years' absence and a distance of 11,500 miles and our reunion became a very ordinary moment.

Leaving the airport was a shock. The intense heat and bright sunshine hit us instantly. Disorientated for a moment, we let Terran lead us to his car, a black Nissan Skyline. He had been a few weeks short of 14 when we had last seen each other but now, looking at him as a young employed adult and living with his fiancée, didn't seem odd at all. Holly, by then a mid-teenager, was still a mixture of little girl and young woman. Spending any time with her would have to wait as Terran took us from the airport to drop her at home. It was hurtful to see her leave the car on her own. Her older brother was on poor terms with her at the time, and for the duration of our stay, apart from a small handful of occasions, the four of us never spent any time together. He stuck rigidly to his decision and refused, even for the two weeks of our stay, to share any time as a family. Eddy and I had to divide our time between both of them.

With both children, we did ordinary things. The patterns we developed while they lived in England continued with a seamless transition between countries and elapsed time. Shopping, visiting family and a little sightseeing all slotted into the familiar rhythm we'd had before they left England. On one or two occasions, I even spent the night with Holly at the family home. When this happened, Derek went to stay with his wife. They'd been separated for a while.

To my shock and dismay, I discovered life been neither ideal nor happy for the children. Derek's wife had been suffering from a mental health condition which caused her to display controlling behaviour and violent outbursts of anger. She had verbally and physically assaulted both children, which had led to Holly going to live temporarily with one of her uncles. It also pushed Terran to leave home. He didn't want his father to know his address in case it led to an unwelcome visit from his stepmother. Had I known any of that, I would have brought them both back to England in an instant. The happy letters Holly sent had been dictated by their stepmother and she would listen in on any phone calls we had to make sure they were telling me how good their lives were. In truth, they'd both suffered emotional and physical abuse.

The environmental and cultural differences were fascinating. Many of the trees had thick, spongy barks and the ones along the verges close to where Holly lived were hung with flat pods the size and shape of bananas. We saw wild cockatoos, kangaroos and giant anthills that stood shoulder height to me. The call of cicadas was relentless and nonstop. The only change in volume was it occasionally increased for a short time as the native insects shouted their mating calls. On our first night there, I was kept awake by the sound of bumping and scraping. I thought the neighbours were moving furniture but learned the next morning that it was possums. They spent their days asleep and crawled down the cavities in the walls at night to hunt for food.

Never having been further than Europe before, I found it very strange how quickly nightfall came. It seemed to take about 15 minutes from the first signs of dusk to complete darkness, yet it stayed hot. Christmas Day was typically Australian, a barbecue in the garden, and Boxing Day was spent with Chris, one of Derek's brothers, who had invited me and Eddy to join him and his wife with their other brother, Denny, and his wife Elaine for the afternoon. Being around so many former in-laws made it the strangest day of the whole stay. Derek spent New Year's Eve with his wife so I went to see Holly. There was a pool in the garden and Eddy and I had a midnight swim. He fell asleep in an armchair soon afterwards.

The two weeks passed quickly. We stayed at the house Terran shared with his fiancée most of the time. At the time, he was working as an upholsterer for a firm that made physiotherapy equipment. His manager, the company owner, had allowed him as much time off work as he wanted while we were with him. Taking us in to meet his workmates and look around the premises, it was obvious how much they thought of him. He also took us to a koala sanctuary which was in woodland and the coolness beneath the trees was very refreshing in the heat. Even though winter was approaching, it was still much hotter and drier than the warmest of English summers.

We used public transport when we went out with Holly and used the bus to get to Brisbane or, as everyone called it, 'the City'. It was there I first saw wild ibises, birds I'd only ever seen before in Ancient Egyptian art. We passed buskers, which were also common in England but the ones we saw were native Australians covered in body paint and playing didgeridoos. Edmund had his own money and enjoyed browsing the gift shops. He got on well with Holly and wanted to buy her a mouse from the large pet shop we liked to wander round. Watching them interact together as though no time or distance had passed between them brought back the feelings of peace I'd experienced that day in the summer before they left, when the children were all playing on Cardboard Hill in the sun.

Given the newness of everything, Edmund surprised me with his behaviour. Throughout the weeks we were there and on all stages of the journeys to Australia and home again, he coped well with everything. The close bond we had was unaffected by the time we spent with the brother and sister he had no memory of and he accepted two strangers calling me Mum without challenging it.

The return journey came around very quickly. We had an uncomfortable family meal the evening before our flight. Terran was still angry with Holly from months earlier and she sulked for the entire time we were in the restaurant. Both children came to the airport to see us off, which was something I insisted on. Despite his reluctance to go anywhere with his sister, my elder son agreed.

The photograph I took of them while we waited at the check-in queue was one I would reprint many times to give as gifts to my family on our return.

It was time to get a job. The visit to Australia had been expensive and my credit card bill was enormous. So was my mobile phone bill as I'd used it to ring home to check on the wellbeing of our dog, who was with a neighbour. There was also something else to consider: Holly wanted to come back to England and my house only had two bedrooms. It would need a loft conversion to make room for her. Everything took a lot longer to plan and when she finally came over, a few days after her 17th birthday, work hadn't even started. I gave her my bedroom and spent six months sleeping on the sofa. When she came, so did Terran and their father. It was less than two weeks before Christmas. Derek was staying with one of his sisters and Terran shared Ed's room.

The transition for Eddy, who had effectively been an only child, was difficult. He had to adjust to life with his siblings and it was getting stressful. Tension between Holly and Edmund had been growing and it came to a head on Christmas Eve. Holly had telephoned Derek. She was crying. I could only hear her side of the conversation but it appeared he'd been telling her he knew it was a mistake and he was taking her back to Australia. I took the phone from her. He told me he knew it would be a disaster. I said plainly, "They need time to settle down."

When I heard Derek say it was his family I retaliated. "Not in my house it isn't." One thing I learned from my years of dealing with difficult behaviour was to stand my ground. A physical fight broke out between Holly and Edmund, resulting in both of them sitting on the landing crying. He had a cut lip from a punch his sister had thrown. Terran became very distressed so I sent him up the road to a friend's house. Before I left to join him, I stood over them.

"Right, I'm going out and I'm not coming home till you've sorted this out," I said.

After that evening, the relationship between my daughter and younger son settled down and they eventually became very close, but something else was about to happen that would change our lives forever.

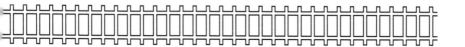

CHAPTER 24

The move from Holly House was getting closer and I was desperately keen for the transition back into mainstream education to go smoothly for Edmund. Earlier in the year, he had been assessed by an educational psychologist to pursue a diagnosis of Asperger's syndrome. This had long been seen as a high-functioning variant of autism. This opinion has, in recent years, been challenged more often, especially within the autistic community itself. At that time and since, professional awareness appeared to be way behind the lived experience of autistic individuals. My own knowledge and understanding of autism was limited, but I was open to anything that would properly explain the challenges Ed had faced from his early childhood.

Despite much progress through trial and error of coping strategies, the meltdowns and violent outbursts had remained. I had spent an hour or so explaining Edmund's behaviour to the educational psychologist. He then spent some time with Ed, who was by then 11 years old. Two weeks later, we returned for the outcome of the assessment, which had taken into account reports from school. He concluded Edmund couldn't be autistic because, as he said, "He can talk and knows what patronising means." It was frustrating and disappointing. On the way home, I asked Edmund about his session with the educational psychologist. "But Mum, he was patronising," he said.

The school move was going to happen regardless of anything else and I was afraid of how Edmund might cope with the transition from a small semi-rural school to a large comprehensive. The opinion of the educational psychologist had been many months earlier and I was dissatisfied with the outcome. With this in mind, I decided to do some research of my own. I conducted internet searches and found huge swathes of books, many written by autistic authors. This fascinated me. The only experience I'd had until then was through a little boy at the Family Support Centre and I'd concluded autism was something to do with little non-verbal boys who sat in corners rocking and occasionally having fits of thrashing around and screaming.

Television documentaries on autism almost exclusively featured men or boys with extraordinary savant abilities. They never featured women or girls, yet there among the many books were authors who were not only adult but female. I ordered information sheets and three books to begin my reading with. These books were all written by autistic people and could have easily been my own life biographies. It was shocking but everything I read and researched made perfect sense. One of the authors described a lonely, solitary childhood filled with imaginary friends, secret diaries and a love of horses and the Wild West. They all spoke about never really fitting in or feeling comfortable in their environments. They spoke about mimicking the behaviour of others while all the time having no sense of belonging.

Could I actually be autistic? I needed to find out. More than anything else, I needed to know who I was and how it might help my sons. It made sense. Even then, autism had been identified as being more prevalent in some families. If I was autistic, then my sons would be too. We shared so many similar traits. It also explained why and how I'd naturally tuned into Terran from birth and the adaptations I'd made to fit the home environment to his needs. It also explained the startling similarities between the half-brothers. Their behaviour hadn't been the result of an inadequate mother, their common factor, but of a sensitive, empathic, caring and autistic one.

Working through the advice given on the information sheets, I made a list of reasons why I thought I had Asperger's syndrome and took them to the family doctor. She listened and then made a referral to a psychologist. During the waiting period, I was haunted by voices from my childhood and adolescent years, voices from my mum, her mum and other members of her family. Why do you always have to have something wrong with you? Why do you talk funny? Why do you talk so slowly? Why can't you be the same as everyone else? Why can't you be more like a little girl instead of a little boy? Why can't you be more like your sister? Why can't you just be normal?

Perhaps they were right, those voices. Maybe I did want 'something to be wrong with me'. Other voices argued back. There was nothing wrong about autism. There was nothing wrong in being autistic. I started my research for my son, not for me. I wanted to help him and in doing so had potentially discovered the 'why' behind the pain, suffering and loneliness that had woven a path through my life.

The answers came two weeks after the appointment with the psychologist. Holly came with me. I was autistic. I was 44 years old. When asked what she thought about me being diagnosed, she said, "She's still my mum." Eight months later, Edmund was finally diagnosed. Two years after that, when Terran was living back in England, he too was diagnosed.

I could have been sitting on a rearward seat of a train, watching raindrops race diagonally down the window. Loneliness had been my oldest friend. I remembered the nights, as even a young child, when I'd cried myself to sleep and woken with tears in my eyes before they opened in the morning. I remembered the years of verbal and physical assaults from my parents. I used to look at other people and their families with an overwhelming longing to be accepted, to belong in such a loving, warm and accepting environment as theirs. To have a family who could laugh together on the couch of friendship would have been the finest thing.

Then I thought of my children. I thought of Terran and Holly with their Australian accents and strong sibling bond. Holly had always been the one to laugh most easily and Terran the most intense and serious of my children. Edmund, the tall dark one who had, by default, created the kind of parent in me I could have never thought possible.

The family I always wanted to be part of was the one I'd grown myself.

ABOUT THE AUTHOR

Laurie Morgen is a UK-based social entrepreneur, speaker and trainer. She designs and delivers autism training workshops to educators, health and social care professionals, parents and anyone with a social conscience.

The second of four children, Laurie always knew she was different but grew up, as she described, with loneliness as her best friend. When she became a parent, Laurie wanted something for her children she had rarely experienced herself: to grow up knowing what it was to be loved unconditionally, to look back as adults to a childhood of warmth and happy memories.

After her diagnosis of Asperger's syndrome in 2006, Laurie went to university and graduated with a 2:1 degree in Journalism from Sheffield Hallam University. Halfway through her degree, Laurie went to an international autism conference and found there was only one main stage autistic speaker. She looked at him and thought 'that's what I want to do'. She has been on many speaker training boot camps and is a member of the Professional Speaking Association.

Laurie has three children and four grandchildren. She lives with four cats, three dogs, two gerbils, a hamster and two budgerigars. She is no longer lonely.